IMAGINING EVIL

# IMAGINING EVIL

## Brian Horne

DARTON · LONGMAN + TODD

First published in 1996 by
Darton, Longman and Todd Ltd
1 Spencer Court
140–142 Wandsworth High Street
London SW18 4JJ

ISBN 0–232–52161–1

A catalogue record for this book is available
from the British Library


Phototypeset in 10/13 Bembo by Intype London Ltd
Printed and bound in Great Britain by
Page Bros, Norwich

For Christopher

# ACKNOWLEDGEMENTS

This book has grown out of a series of lectures delivered under the sponsorship of the Montgomery Trust. I should like to thank the members of the Trust and its Director for their support in the publication of them in this form.

Thanks are due to the following for permission to quote copyright material: Cambridge University Press for *Augustine on Evil* by G. R. Evans; T & T Clark for *Church Dogmatics* by Karl Barth; David Higham Associates for *He Came Down from Heaven* and *The Image of the City and Other Essays* by Charles Williams; Penguin Books Ltd for *Candide* by Voltaire, translated by John Butt, *City of God* by Augustine, translated by H. Bettenson, edited by D. Knowles and *The Plague* by Albert Camus, translated by Stuart Gilbert.

# CONTENTS

FOREWORD ix

1. THE PROBLEM POSED: A MYTH OF ORIGINS 1

2. JOB'S COMPLAINT: THE APPEARANCE OF SATAN 12

3. 'I SAW SATAN FALL LIKE LIGHTNING' 23

4. DOES A SHADOW EXIST? 34

5. MEDIEVAL TRANSFORMATIONS 46

6. THE RETURN OF SATAN: 'EVIL BE THOU MY GOOD' 62

7. EVERYTHING FOR THE BEST 76

8. EVIL ROMANTICISED: THE LURE OF DEPRAVITY 89

9. RETURNING TO EDEN: GOOD AS EVIL 104

AFTERWORD 124

NOTES 133

INDEX 139

# CONTENTS

# FOREWORD

*It is the role of the imagination to re-map the world.*

Edward Bond

Wᴇ ᴀʟʟ ʜᴀᴠᴇ need of maps to find our way in the world. Our apprehension of reality is fragmentary and confusing; our knowledge of the world we inhabit and our sense of our place in that world is uncertain. At times our experience of life is characterised by confidence and hope, at others times by incomprehension and alienation. One moment there is order, the next moment there is chaos. We may be in possession of all the information we need and yet not be able to make sense of it. We may have obtained all the necessary facts of our existence but still have no way of seeing how they relate to one another, what they mean or what to do with them. The world has to be interpreted; we seem to have no direct, intuitive grasp on reality. We lose our way. As individual centres of consciousness and self-awareness we live our lives in relation to a world of objects outside of ourselves, but the exact relationship is often problematic: the exterior arena of objects can be opaque and mysterious to the interior world of our own sense of ourselves.

And so we interpret the world by various means, giving it comprehensible order: we make maps and rely on the maps of others. Every word, every picture, every conversation, every song, provides us with clues to the shape and meaning of the universe we inhabit and our own place in it. Imagining is a distinctive way of being related to the facts of our existence, a special way of mapping the world. It is not the only way; there also is the way of the intellect: the attempt to make sense of reality by imposing on it patterns of rational analysis – whether they are the words of philosophers or the symbols of the mathematician.

In a lecture of 1952, 'Art and Society', Paul Tillich addressed the question of the role of the artist in both the shaping of culture and the formation of the individual: 'Man wants to participate in other beings . . . Knowledge is one of these ways. Through cognitive participation, the individual self takes into itself its world. Where there is knowledge there is participation.' But having said this, he noted that there was something lacking in this definition of participation. Sheer knowledge, a cognitive seizing of the facts of existence, left the individual aware of an incompleteness, a sense of unfulfilment, a sense that there is still more to know, or, rather, that participation in something beyond oneself required knowledge of a different kind: 'there is a way of penetrating into the hidden quality of the thing and this way is artistic creation. All the arts penetrate into the depths of things which are beyond the reach of cognition.'[1]

Tillich does not discuss the imagination here but it is impossible to consider the work of the artist without assuming the function of the imagination. The imagination is the way in which the internal world of the perceiving subject participates in the external world is grasped and interiorised by the internal world of the individual human being. What may be said of things may also be said of ideas. And this is where we see another role for the imagination to play. It not only forges the link between the interior world of the individual person and the exterior world of objects, it acts as an integrating agent within the human being, bringing together the often separate, sometimes conflicting forces of intellect and emotion. It creates images, aural and visual, that enable the union of head and heart to take place. It helps to establish integrity in human experience.

The intellectual tradition of Western religion is strong – sometimes overpowering. The Christian faith, in particular, has sometimes given the appearance of being little more than a set of propositions, items on an intellectual agenda. The result is that these items have frequently received a kind of formal assent but have hardly been taken to heart. The subject of evil offers itself as an interesting illustration, for it has, more often than not, been treated at this level of the propositional – as a problem posed in philosophical terms which has to be solved by the means of rational argument. I have approached the matter from a different angle; not ignoring the necessity of the rational, philosophical examination of the subject, but trying to set it in the context of the way the imagination (and many individual imaginations) has apprehended this mystery. The truths of religion, evil included, need to be embodied in forms created by the imagination before they can be laid hold upon and become meaningful to the human being. The baroque paintings and sculpture of sixteenth-century Italy will convey truths to the viewer that all the readings of the proceedings of the Council of Trent will never convey; T. S. Eliot's *Four Quartets* will awaken in the reader an awareness of the nature of religious experience that no textbook on the psychology of religion could ever provide. (In the midst of his discussion of evil in his *Church Dogmatics* Karl Barth suddenly introduces an excursus on the music of Mozart in order to convey the reality of something which he seems to feel is almost beyond the capacity of rational presentation.)

Reason is essentially reductive, imagination is essentially expansive. This is not to say that one mode is to be preferred to another; it is not 'better' to be an artist than a philosopher; not 'better' to be imaginative than intellectual. Not at all. However, I am trying to make the point that doctrines and theories remain external to us, cold and dead, until they have been grasped by the imagination. But we have also to recognise that the process can be a complex one: sometimes a doctrine or a theory will first be enunciated or propounded in a purely analytical form and will only gradually receive an imagined form; sometimes the imagination will precede the intellect by the provision of a form which will then come to be formulated in an analytical manner. The interplay is continuous.

The aim of this book is a modest one. There is no attempt to give a comprehensive account of the history of the concept of evil in the Christian tradition; such an undertaking would run to several volumes and is, in any case, beyond my competence. Nor am I trying to find an answer to the problem of evil: this is not an exercise in the philosophy of religion. It is merely an attempt to enter the Christian tradition at a number of points along its history and show something of the fascination of that interplay between the intellect and the imagination as they encounter the mystery of iniquity.

# THE PROBLEM POSED:
# A MYTH OF ORIGINS

By the time of his death in 1960 at the age of 46, the French-Algerian writer Albert Camus had acquired an international reputation and an almost mythic status among the young intellectuals of Europe and America. His early novel, *L'Etranger* (*The Outsider*), published in 1942, seemed to young people growing up in the two decades after the Second World War to be a near-perfect expression of their anxieties, fears and disaffections: its theme of the arbitrariness of events and the absurdity of existence mirrored their sense of disillusionment and alienation. His second novel, *La Peste* (*The Plague*), published in 1947, never quite achieved the talismanic status of the first, despite the fact that in some ways it was a more mature work of fiction. The tone was both more austere and more humane, and although 'absurdity' was still a prominent motif, it had undergone a transformation and was placed in a quite different context. It is sometimes said that the novel should be read as a kind of allegory of France during the period of the Occupation, but it is more than that (if it is that); it raises universal philosophical problems and poses them in the harshest way.

The *mise-en-scène* is the port of Oran on the Algerian coast. An epidemic of terrible ferocity has hit the town; and at the centre of the story is the doctor, Rieux, who has to deal with the victims of the plague. There is also a priest, Father Paneloux, described by the author as one who 'had shown himself a stalwart champion of Christian doctrine at its most precise and purest, equally remote from modern laxity and the obscurantism of the past'.[1] So serious has the plague become, and so numerous are the deaths that have occurred, that the priest feels bound to preach about the situation at the Sunday mass:

> If today the plague is in your midst, that is because the hour has struck for taking thought. The just man need have no fear, but the evil-doer has good cause to tremble. For plague is the flail of God and the world is His threshing-floor, and implacably He will thrash out His harvest until the wheat is separated from the chaff. There will be more chaff than wheat, few chosen of the many called. Yet this calamity was willed by God. Too long has this world of ours counted on divine mercy, on God's forgiveness . . . now He has turned His face away from us. And so, God's light withdrawn, we walk in darkness, the thick darkness of this plague.[2]

The argument is familiar and is based upon a particular notion of justice: retribution. Transgression against the laws of God will be punished, sinfulness will incur wrath, evil-doing will result in suffering. Rieux and a friend are found later discussing the sermon. The doctor refuses to accept either the concept of retributive justice or the logic of the priest's argument: the conversation brings the reader near to the philosophical centre of Camus' novel, and perhaps Camus' own position on the mystery of innocent suffering and its relationship to religious belief.

> 'After all,' the doctor repeated, then hesitated again, fixing his eyes on Tarrou, 'it's something that a man of your sort can understand most likely, but, since the order of the world is shaped by death, mightn't it be better for God if we refuse to believe in Him, and struggle with all our might against death,

without raising our eyes towards heaven where He sits in silence?'[3]

This theme too is familiar: in a life that is 'shaped by death' the best one can do is endure the apparent meaninglessness with as much courage as one can summon and refuse to accept theological explanations (which explain nothing) and religious consolations (which give little consolation). The portrayal of Paneloux is not unsympathetic: he is not lacking in courage or compassion; it is not his character that Rieux challenges, but his theology. The epidemic grows worse and the priest joins those who are trying to care for the sick and dying. A day comes when they meet at the bedside of a dying child.

Paneloux gazed down at the small mouth, fouled with the sores of the plague and pouring out the angry death-cry that has sounded through the ages of mankind. He sank on his knees, and all present found it natural to hear him say in a voice hoarse but clearly audible across that nameless, never-ending wail:

'My God, spare this child . . .!' . . . it was over . . . Rieux was already on his way out, walking so quickly and with such a strange look on his face that Paneloux put out an arm to check him when he was about to pass him in the door-way.

'Come, doctor . . .' he began. Rieux swung round on him fiercely. 'Ah! That child, anyhow, was innocent – and you know it as well as I do!'[4]

The only answer the priest can make to this accusation is to say that the mystery of suffering is beyond human understanding, and that, perhaps, we 'should love what we cannot understand'. Rieux refuses the proffered words of consolation and rejects the theology which sustains them. 'No, Father. I've a very different idea of love. And until my dying day I shall refuse to love a scheme of things in which children are put to torture.' The problem, thus, is posed. How is it possible to 'accept' such a scheme of things? What meaning can be found in a universe in which the apparently innocent suffer so outrageously? Whence is the origin of this condition? Is it possible that there is an 'explanation'? Is there, perhaps, something inherently evil about the universe in which we live? If there is, how and why does it arise? Does it enter from outside or is it to be seen as part of the structure of being?

All religions have attempted to provide answers to the questions which have just been asked, for they are the questions which puzzle human beings most deeply; and all religions have begun in the same place, with a myth – in the collective imagination. And because the questions are not peculiar to one society or period of history or culture, the myths which embody the search for meaning often bear certain structural resemblances to one another.

One of the most famous of all myths of origin, and one with which we in the Western European tradition are most familiar, is the ancient Greek myth of Pandora. We are told that the woman called Pandora, made of clay by Hephaestus, was endowed, as her name indicates, with every gift and was presented with a casket. She – a kind of Greek Eve figure – was married to Epimetheus and imprudently opened the box. Immediately there flew out all the evils of mankind. The poet Hesiod wrote:

> Before this time men lived upon the earth
> Apart from sorrow and painful work,
> Free from disease, which brings the Death-gods in.
> But now the woman opened up the cask,
> And scattered pains and evils among men.
> Inside the cask's hard walls remained one thing,
> Hope only, which did not fly through the door.
> The lid stopped her, but all the others flew,

4

> Thousands of troubles, wandering the earth.
> The earth is full of evils, and the sea.[5]

No mention is made here in Hesiod of disobedience, and it is a story which reveals the trickery of the gods; but the implications are plain: temptation is placed deliberately in the way of the human creature, and curiosity is punished. Moreover, it is not only the individual perpetrator of the act who is punished, it is the whole human race that is involved in suffering. There are many differences, of course, between this myth and that which we find in the Hebrew religion and Christianity, but there are also interesting similarities. In the Hebrew-Christian myth we find a man and a woman and an act of imprudence. This myth has a precise location: a garden. 'And the Lord God planted a garden in Eden, in the east; and there he put the man whom he had formed' (Gen. 2:8). The Hebrew and Christian religions do not begin to explain the origin of evil with a theory, a philosophical speculation, but with a story.

We are not concerned here with the factuality of the account in Genesis. It is not our task to claim that Eden was really a place, or that Adam and Eve were really the first human beings to have existed. We are concerned with a different kind of truth: the truth that is known both to poets and to social anthropologists – mythical truth. To the poet it is the truth constructed by the imagination of the individual artist; to the anthropologist it is the truth that emerges from the collective imagination. Joseph Campbell writes:

> Man, apparently, cannot maintain himself in the universe without belief in some arrangement of the general inheritance of myth. In fact, fullness of his life would seem even to stand in a direct ratio to the depth and range not of his rational thought but of his local mythology. Whence the force of these unsubstantial themes, by which they are empowered to galvanize populations,

creating of them civilizations, each with a beauty and self-compelling destiny of its own? And why should it be that whenever men have looked for something solid on which to found their lives, they have chosen not the facts in which the world abounds, but the myths of an immemorial imagination . . .?[6]

No answer has been found to the question which Campbell has raised here, and we simply note the truth of his observations. Later generations were to speculate philosophically on the origin of evil, but in the beginning it was in a myth that the human predicament was conveyed. Northrop Frye comments:

> As a story, a myth becomes a model of human experience, and its relation to that experience becomes a confronting and present experience. The truth of the story of the Fall of Adam and Eve does not depend on the possibility that an archaeologist may eventually dig up their skeletons. It depends on its power to convey to the present sense of alienation in human consciousness, the sense of being surrounded by a nature not ours.[7]

The story that the 'author' of the book of Genesis tells could hardly be simpler in style. It is little more than a plain recitation of 'facts'. According to the second account of creation in Genesis, Adam is created first:

> The Lord God took the man and put him in the garden of Eden to till it and keep it. And the Lord God commanded the man saying 'You may freely eat of every tree of the garden; but of the tree of the knowledge of good and evil you shall not eat, for in the day that you eat of it you shall die' (Gen. 2:15).

No comment is offered on why the fruit of the tree of the knowledge of good and evil is denied to the man; interpretation is not the habit of the mythical style. After this Eve is created.

6

'And the man and his wife were both naked, and were not ashamed' (Gen. 2:25). Even here the observation on their shamelessness is not an interpretative remark, it is a statement of fact, even though a highly significant one, as becomes apparent later in the tale. Then comes the central piece of the narrative: the scene of the temptation and the act of disobedience:

> Now the serpent was more subtle than any other creature that the Lord God had made. He said to the woman, 'Did God say, "You shall not eat of any tree in the garden"?'
>
> And the woman said to the serpent, 'We may eat of the fruit of the trees of the garden; but God said, "You shall not eat of the fruit of the tree which is in the midst of the garden, neither shall you touch it, lest you die."'
>
> But the serpent said to the woman, 'You will not die. For God knows that when you eat of it your eyes will be opened, and you will be like God, knowing good and evil.'
>
> So when the woman saw that the tree was good for food, and a delight to the eyes, and that the tree was to be desired to make one wise, she took of its fruit and ate; and she also gave some to her husband, and he ate. Then the eyes of both were opened; and they knew that they were naked (Gen. 3:1–7).

This myth has played a vital part in Hebrew and Christian self-understanding; it has been the controlling story of anthropology and theology and is deeply embedded in the psyche of the whole of Western civilisation. And how are we to understand it? It is invariably referred to as the myth of the Fall of Man, and John Henry Newman's famous remark that there 'can be no doubt that mankind has been involved in some terrible aboriginal calamity' may be taken as an expression of the orthodox Christian interpretation of the story. But we have already seen that Northrop Frye has a different reading of the text. For him the story is a model of the human experience of alienation

7

and the sense of an indifferent, perhaps hostile, nature surrounding us. This is a reading which sets aside the theological concepts of sin and grace, good and evil; for him it is not a story about the origin of evil at all, it is an indispensable myth of Western culture and can be interpreted in entirely existential terms. And a radical reinterpretation of the myth has recently been offered by the Old Testament scholar James Barr in his Read-Tuckwell lectures:

> my argument is that, taken in itself and for itself, this narrative is not, as it has commonly been understood in our tradition, basically a story of the origins of sin and evil, still less a depiction of absolute evil or total depravity; it is a story of how human immortality was almost gained, but in fact was lost.[8]

There is no indication in the texts of the Old Testament themselves, Barr argues, for saying that the Hebrew religion traced the origin of human wickedness to this primeval story of Adam and Eve: the seriousness of sin and the existence of evil are, of course, constantly alluded to, but neither sin nor evil is caused by an original act of disobedience on the part of 'our first parents'. That particular reading of the myth – a sudden 'drastic and catastrophic change by which the human relationship with God was ruined' – arises much later in Judaism; and in Christianity it is associated with the writings of St Paul.

Many would want to question Barr's interpretation of the Hebrew tradition, but few could argue with his representation of Paul's position. One of the most striking of all the apostle's images is the image of Jesus Christ as the Second Adam: the one who redeems the human race from the state of helplessness, despair and imprisonment caused by the First Adam's sin: 'For as by a man came death, by a man has also come the resurrection of the dead. For as in Adam all die, so also in Christ shall all be made alive' (1 Cor. 15:21). Paul argues that sin enters the world through Adam, and with sin, death. In his reading of the Paradise myth sin and death are closely connected. Death is seen, specifically, as the consequence of sin: the disobedience of Adam brings about the destruction of the harmonious relationship with God and the ruin of the human race. What Paul does not discuss in relation to the story of the garden of Eden is the notion of evil: his focus is on sin and death which are never described by him as 'evil'. He speaks elsewhere of the 'mystery of iniquity' (2 Thess. 2:7) and seems, more often than not, to see evil as a supernatural force, but never suggests that one should read the story of Adam and Eve as a story which has anything to tell us about the existence of supernatural evil. The Pauline interpretation of the story came to dominate the Christian readings of the myth, especially in the West, as we shall see later.

It is interesting to note that, if this is the interpretation of the Genesis myth that one prefers, one is seeing in it a meaning that is closer to that of the Pandora myth than to that in the readings of Northrop Frye or James Barr. In the myth of Pandora's box the connection between the actions of the woman and the sufferings of the whole of mankind is made very precisely; even death might be the result of the opening of this casket. The passage from Hesiod suggests it:

> Before this time men lived upon the earth
> Apart from sorrow and painful work,
> Free from disease which brings the Death-gods in.

The parallels with the Hebrew story are quite striking:

To the woman he said, 'I will greatly multiply your pain in child-bearing, in pain you shall bring forth children' . . . And to Adam he said, 'Because you have listened to the voice of your wife, and have eaten of the tree of which I commanded you, "You shall not eat of it", cursed is the ground because of you; in toil you shall eat of it all the days of your life; thorns and thistles it shall bring forth to you . . . you are dust and to dust you shall return' (Gen. 3:16).

Where the stories differ is in their moral content. The demigods Epimetheus and Pandora are morally neutral and they are not judged for their actions; the actions of the human Adam and Eve are morally reprehensible and they are judged. They are held personally responsible for their wilful disobedience to the divine command. As Christian theology developed, they were to be held responsible for the universal alienation of humanity from God and, in some schemes, for that 'bias towards evil' which is the condition, according to some theologians, of Original Sin.

There are several questions which the myth leaves open and unanswered. Perhaps the most puzzling is: why did Adam and Eve act as they did? Here we encounter the mysterious fourth figure in the story, the tempter. He is described simply as the 'serpent'. There is no indication, in the text, that the reader should regard him as a supernatural force or the embodiment of evil, which he became in many later Christian interpretations. He certainly tempts Eve with his seductive talk of knowledge and power, but she is not compelled to listen to him or to believe that he is telling the truth. Neither Adam nor Eve is in thrall to him in any way; they are free to choose and act as they will. They do, in fact, sin, because they knowingly disobey the command of God, but the story does not show them to be grasped by a power beyond themselves and which might be identified as evil. The cause of their action lies wholly within themselves.

Later ages were to interpret their behaviour as a submission to the devil and the moment at which the harmonious order of the universe fell apart: the Genesis myth was seen as a genuine portrayal of the origin of evil. Henceforward the world was to be a battle-ground between the forces of good and those of evil and everything would be subject to decay, suffering and death. The sin of Adam will be held to account for everything, from human malice to volcanic eruptions; from the death-camps of Hitler's Germany to plagues of locusts. Dr Rieux's sad scepticism about the meaning of life and his angry questioning of the concept of a just and loving God in the face of the fact of innocent suffering will become a constant theme in Christian history and will be answered by a recitation of the myth of the Fall. No other myth will have such power over the religious imagination or receive such a variety of interpretations.

# JOB'S COMPLAINT:
# THE APPEARANCE OF SATAN

THE MOST FAMOUS of all moral fables in the Hebrew–Christian tradition begins like a fairy-tale: 'There was once a man in the land of Uz whose name was Job.' In these spare opening words a mythic quality is immediately given to the story. We are in the world of folk-memory: the story we are about to hear is the story of Everyman, as well as the story of Job; it is our story; and it has intrigued and puzzled centuries of readers in ways that few other books have done. No matter that there might have been a land called Uz, or that Job's sons and daughters have names: this is neither a history nor a novel. The place could be anywhere on earth, the characters could be anybody.

There is no attempt at psychological depth in the brief narrative nor any effort at representing reality. A few verses paint the picture of Job's initial state of wealth and blessedness: 'This man was blameless and upright, one who feared God and turned away from evil . . . This man was the greatest of all the people of the east.' Then there is an abrupt change of scene and we find ourselves in the court of heaven where 'the sons of God' are 'presenting' themselves before the Almighty. Satan is among them and a dialogue beings. God asks, 'Have you considered my servant Job?' In response to Satan's sceptical assessment of Job's goodness God gives Job into Satan's power. Will Job remain godly when he has lost everything? Will he continue to worship the Almighty when all that he treasured has been stripped away from him?

And so all is taken: sheep and cattle, houses, children and health. He is advised by his wife to 'Curse God and die', but he refused in words that have become etched into the Hebrew-Christian imagination: 'Naked I came from my mother's womb, and naked I shall return there: the Lord gave, and the Lord has taken away: blessed be the name of the Lord.' In his steadfast refusal to 'blame' God for anything that has occurred he has passed the test and remains innocent. The victory, it appears, is God's, and Job is rewarded for his constancy, at the end of the story, with the complete restitution of all his former happiness and prosperity. But the end of the story is forty chapters away, and in the intervening pages a very different and perplexing picture emerges.

It is hardly surprising that the book of Job should have entered so deeply into the heart and mind of our culture, for its subject is the deepest and darkest of all human mysteries: the mystery of the suffering of the innocent; that problem for religious faith so searingly exposed by Albert Camus in the character of Dr Rieux in *The Plague*. Job, like Rieux, asks the question: Whence this suffering? What is its cause? Far from submitting passively to the will of God (the picture given in the narrative of the folk-tale), Job, in speech after speech, brings his case to the bar of the court of heaven in angry self-justification, protesting his innocence and demanding to know the reason for his affliction. He does not merely ask to be delivered from suffering – that is not the main thrust of his complaint – he asks primarily for the meaning of his suffering to be shown.

Carl Gustav Jung, who was fascinated by the story of Job, wrote late in his life, 'Meaninglessness inhibits fullness of life and is therefore equivalent to illness. Meaning makes a great many things endurable – perhaps everything.'[1] There is in Job's speeches precisely this search for meaning: the suggestion that all the suffering he experiences could be endured if he could discover why it is that he is undergoing this ordeal. How can he, in his innocence of life and careful observance of all the duties of his religion, have deserved the calamities that have been visited on him? His words echo down the centuries in the cries of all those who can see no reason for their sorrows, who ask, like Job, only for meaning, so that their pain can be endured:

> know then that God has put me in the wrong
> and closed his net around me.
> Even when I cry out 'Violence!' I am not answered;
> I call aloud, but there is no justice.
> He has walled up my way so that I cannot pass,
> and he has set darkness upon my paths.
> He has stripped my glory from me, and taken the
> crown from my head.
>
> (Job 19:6)

He is visited by friends who offer him 'comfort' by trying to give him an explanation for the catastrophe he has suffered. In this they are doing exactly what he is requiring: they will give meaning to what has happened. The fault, they argue, lies within Job himself, though Job does not recognise it. He will find the explanation in his own wickeness. He cannot blame God for anything, for God is just.

> Does God pervert justice?
> Or does the Almighty pervert the right? . . .
> if you are pure and upright, then he will rouse
>     himself for you
> and restore to you your rightful place.
>
> (Job 8:5)

Job will not accept their conventional interpretation of justice and their simple equation of goodness with prosperity and wickedness with punishment; and he expands his vision to include the whole world in his complaint. It is not only himself who is innocent: humanity cries out to God that the wicked prosper and the righteous are broken on the wheel of affliction. His bitter reproach reaches its crescendo in chapter 24:

> Why are times not kept by the Almighty,
> and why do those who know him never see his days? . . .
> From the city the dying groan, and the throat of the
>    wounded cries for help;
> yet God pays no attention to their prayer.

Here Job questions the very notion of the justice of God. In a universe where children die of starvation and the powerful can impose their will by violence, how is it possible to speak of the justice of the Almighty or argue that there is a moral order in the universe? Job's dilemma is the dilemma of all who believe that the Creator of the world is a God whose nature is to be defined in terms, not only of power, but also of justice and love: the God of all Jews, Christians and Muslims. If God is all-powerful he seems not to care about the sufferings of the innocent: goodness and evil are equally irrelevant to the exercise of his capricious will. The horrifying bleakness of this vision of reality was to be dramatised centuries later by Shakespeare in *King Lear*, bound upon his 'wheel of fire'. 'As flies to wanton boys are we to the gods: / They kill us for their sport.'[2]

If this is true, it is impossible to speak of the justice of God. On the other hand, if he cares for their sufferings but is unable to do anything to alleviate their pain, he cannot be said to be all-powerful; and the question then arises, where does the suffering come from? Is there evil in the universe over which God has no control? Is there some supernatural principle of evil opposed to the power and love of God which may be held to be responsible for the misery of man and the disorder of creation? And could that principle be identified as Satan? It would be a tidy answer to the dilemma, but it is not an answer that is acceptable to Hebrew-Christian theology, nor is it an answer that can be read off the pages of the book of Job. The universe of Job is uncompromisingly monistic: there is no force capable of withstanding the power of the Lord, no principle of evil exterior to his creation. The name 'Satan' is merely a term for an 'accuser': a kind of prosecutor. Whatever later ages may have made of the figure of Satan, here, in Job, it is quite clear that Satan is a servant – if a somewhat sardonic servant – perhaps even a 'son'. He is permitted by the Almighty to test the man Job. We cannot escape the dilemma: the focus returns to God and the questionable nature of his being.

The three 'comforters' offer the argument that is to be found over and over again in the writings of the Old Testament. If evil exists, God has allowed it and punishes evildoing. Human beings will be held to account for their sins. What other meaning can be given to the concept of justice? Goodness will, moreover, be rewarded. The lesson is driven home by the prophets and law-givers alike. Obey the commands of God if you would be blessed, and your blessing will not only be a kind of inward spiritual peace, it will be material security and prosperity. At the very beginning of the Hebrews' history God enters into a covenant with his people, promising a land flowing with milk and honey; but to receive this land they must abide by the conditions of the contract. Failure to do so will result in destruction. This is classically expounded in Deuteronomy, the book which is at the heart of Jewish law:

> For the Lord your God is bringing you into a good land, a land
> with flowing streams, with springs and underground waters
> welling up in valleys and hills, a land of wheat and barley, of

vines and fig trees and pomegranates, a land of olive trees and honey, a land where you may eat bread without scarcity, where you will lack nothing . . . But remember the Lord your God, for it is he who gives you power to get wealth . . . If you forget the Lord your God and follow other gods and worship them, I solemnly warn you today that you shall surely perish (Deut. 8:7).

Eliphaz the Temanite, Bildad the Shuhite and Zophar the Naamathite do nothing more than repeat this classical doctrine of God's dealing with his people. After all, had not the prophets constantly warned the citizens of Samaria that their apostasy would cause the downfall of their city, and did not Jerusalem itself fall to the armies of Babylon on account of the faithlessness of Judah? Why should Job suppose that the justice of God had changed; that there was now no correlation between transgression and punishment, virtue and reward? In blunt colloquial terms, you reap what you sow; you must expect to pay for what you do. The only trouble is that it does not seem to be true; life simply does not work like that – as Job angrily points out, citing his own misery as an example.

Our own experience of life confirms Job's complaint; but before we go any further, we should recognise that no theory of justice, divine or human, can exclude the notion that virtue should be rewarded and wickedness punished. This idea is not peculiar to the religion and society of the Jewish people; it is not even invented by them. It is, for example, a fundamental principle of Greek and Roman law. All judicial systems are concerned with establishing innocence and guilt and dealing with those states appropriately; the innocent will be exonerated (the virtuous will be rewarded) and the guilty will be punished (the wicked will suffer). It could even be argued that such a concept of justice is universal to humanity – so long as there is a concept of justice at all. To believe in a moral universe is to believe that there is a necessary relation between the rightness or wrongness of actions (however that may be defined) and the rewards or punishments that follow. The argument that there is not, nor ever could be such a relation is an argument for a chaotic universe and an absurd existence. This is, to some degree, the position of Dr Rieux in *The Plague*. The explanation offered by the priest, Paneloux, for the agonising deaths of small children is rejected by the doctor: the universe seems to have no moral structure, and life, in the end, becomes absurd. If there is a divinity, it is one that is impervious to our understanding; the mystery of iniquity remains unfathomable.

There is a 'fourth comforter' in Job, the young man Elihu, who tries to find another way out of the dilemma. In his speeches he asks Job to approach his misfortune from a different angle and in so doing anticipates the speeches of God in the closing chapters:

> For God speaks in one way,
> and in two, though man does not perceive it.
> In a dream, in a vision of the night,
> when deep sleep falls upon men,
> while they slumber on their beds,
> then he opens the ears of men,
> and terrifies them with warnings.

(Job 33:14–16)

The search for meaning and justice is diverted into a fresh channel by Elihu. Is there not a positive value in suffering – whether it is deserved or not? When this truth is grasped the disasters that have overtaken the unhappy sufferer can be turned into a means of good: suffering that is accepted with patience and humility bends the will of the creature to that of the Creator and brings him to moral perfection:

> Man is also chastened with pain upon his bed,
> and with continual strife in his bones . . .
> Behold, God does all these things,
> twice, three times, with a man,
> to bring back his soul from the Pit,
> that he may see the light of life.
>
> (Job 33:19, 29–30)

The guilt or innocence of Job is no longer the issue; innocent suffering is not to be considered an evil, it is to be seen as the instrument for the purification of the soul.

Faced with the apparent injustices of life and the mystery of undeserved pain, preachers, theologians and mystics have, for centuries, embraced this doctrine and exhorted their followers to submit quietly and patiently to the blows they have received; not merely in the belief that what is lost or endured in this life will be gained and compensated for in the next, but also in the belief that these blows are necessary for the shaping of the spirit; carving them by tribulation into new and better shapes; bringing them eventually to a state of moral perfection and union with the divine.

Moreover, there is clear biblical precedent for this teaching – not only in the book of Job, but particularly in the New Testament. 'For what credit is it, if when you do wrong and are beaten for it you take it patiently? But if when you do right and suffer for it you take it patiently, you have God's approval' (1 Pet. 2:20). Even more emphatic is the author of the epistle to the Hebrews, who warns his readers to expect to endure suffering at the hands of God: 'My child, do not regard lightly the discipline of the Lord . . . for the Lord disciplines those whom he loves, and chastises every child whom he accepts' (Heb. 12:5).

It cannot be denied that this belief, so deeply ingrained in the Christian tradition, has been a source of a great solace and wonderful strength in the lives of countless men and women down the centuries, nor can it be denied that the patient acceptance of pain and misfortune has generated remarkable courage and sweetness in the most terrible circumstances; and if this belief is accepted it neatly disposes of the view that innocent suffering is somehow 'evil' and intolerable. Though, it does not in itself provide an argument for saying that the cause could be found in a source other than God: God could allow such misery to occur, knowing that properly endured, it would become part of the process of spiritual perfection.

But it must also be recognised that this understanding also raises grave difficulties. To most people there is a profound offensiveness in the presentation of this picture of God: our existential experience is that many human beings are 'ground down' by misery. It seems simply a lie to maintain that all suffering is potentially ennobling in every circumstance. Some people become less human very often. They are imprisoned by experiences of injustice or persecution: they are made vicious and become degraded. In these cases it is impossible to extricate the problem of innocent suffering from the problem of evil, as the viciousness and degradation is experienced as an outrage, a contradiction of the loving purposes of God.

Finally there is the puzzle of the closing chapters of the book: God's answer to Job. Before the terse conclusion of the story – a formal coda in fairy-tale style – God, at last, 'appears' and speaks. The complaint has been heard: it will be answered. But the words which are uttered seem to bear no relation to the questions which have been asked; and, setting aside Job's bitter reproaches, God admonishes his creature with an accusatory question: 'I will question, and you shall declare to me' (Job 38:3). What follows, in page after page of splendid poetry, is a theophany: a revelation of the magnificence of the Creator as displayed in the wonders of the natural world: 'Where were you when I laid the foundation of the earth? . . . who laid its cornerstone, when the morning stars sang together, and all the sons of God shouted for joy?'

It is glorious, but it is not an answer; and I remain unconvinced by the many commentators who have tried to 'justify' God in these extraordinary speeches. Better rather the cold comfort of Elihu than the disingenuous piety of a statement like: 'Job now comes to see that in the face of the quite baffling complexity of the human situation, the proper behaviour of man was to be humbly silent, in the quiet assurance that the moral government of the world was safe in the hands of God.'[3] Job does indeed reply humbly in the face of this overwhelming vision: 'I have uttered what I did not understand . . . and repent in dust and ashes' (Job 42:6). But his words only reinforce the suggestion that the questions which have so troubled him have been declared invalid, beyond the reach of human understanding; that God's action is arbitrary and cannot be judged by any human measure: a theological position which is contradicted in other parts of the Bible, where God declares himself as a God whose justice can be relied upon. But here the hubris of human complaint has been annihilated by the exercise of divine power. Justice itself loses meaning in this arena. In a less merciful religion, where the gods are more capricious and the fate that rules the world is inexorable in its operation, the man who thus contended with divinity would himself have been annihilated; here at least his humility and repentance are accepted and his life is restored. But there is no 'solution', there is only submission to the inexplicable facts.

The theology of the book of Job runs through into a book of a very different kind: Ecclesiastes, a book in which a devout resignation pervades the atmosphere and a sense of agnosticism before the deep mysteries of life hangs in the air:

> What has been is what will be,
> and what has been done is what will be done;

and there is nothing new under the sun.

(Eccles. 1:9)

There are no theophanies here, no revelation of the terrifying majesty of God nor any attempt to deal with the mystery of iniquity. Evil is simply woven, inevitably, into the fabric of existence. 'Like fish which are taken in an evil net, and like birds which are caught in a snare, so the sons of men are snared for an evil time, when it suddenly falls upon them' (Eccles. 9:12). Evil is not even located in a moral perspective here. Meaninglessness and death are constant companions in life. Why raise questions for which one cannot find the answer? Futility haunts all our endeavours and extinction undoes our sense of ourselves. The only difference between us and the animals is that we know that we are mortal and they do not; we count the days and they cannot. But the counting is a fruitless activity, for we can change nothing, and the knowledge of mutability only brings a bitter wisdom. An ironical submission is the best that we, as humans, can hope to achieve.

Can this be the end of the story? The history of Judaism and Christianity and of Western European civilisation as a whole says not, and shows in every generation a refusal to accept the answer which is no answer. In the horrors of the Nazi concentration camps and the purges of Stalinist Russia the question of Job was still being asked – 'Why?' And the figure of Satan, so artfully introduced as a literary device in the book of Job, was to take new and strange shapes in the centuries that followed.

# 'I SAW SATAN FALL
# LIKE LIGHTNING'

FOUR HUNDRED MILES south of Paris, in the region of France between the Pyrenees and the Rhone still known as Languedoc, is the city of Albi – famous not only for its food and its cathedral but for having given its name to a religious sect which presented the medieval Church with one of its most serious challenges. The Albigensian sect seems to have appeared quite suddenly at the beginning of the twelfth century in this civilised land already rich in a vernacular literature and courtly life, but it spread rapidly across southern France and northern Italy, attracting many people to its semi-secret rituals and doctrines. As early as 1150 the Catholic Church realised it was confronting a for-midable opponent and tried, by every means at its disposal, to counter its influence and prevent its spread. When mission after mission of teachers and preachers proved to be ineffectual and the hostility of the Albigensians to the Church grew more open as it gained momentum, Pope Innocent III appealed to the secular powers. Under the leadership of Simon de Montfort, French armies attacked the towns and villages known to have Albigensian sympathies in the first decade of the thirteenth century. The ferocity of the attempted suppression of the heresy has made the Albigensian Crusade one of the most infamous episodes of Christian history, but that the Church should have acted in this way dramatically illustrates the seriousness with which it regarded the teachings of the sect and the power of its attraction.

What it saw was a version of Christian teaching which was an imaginative perversion of the gospel. In a memorable phrase Charles Williams, in his history of the Christian Church, *The Descent of the Dove*, referred to a 'waft of death' going out from Albi in the twelfth century; and the Church recognised it immediately, for what was happening in the unique culture of Languedoc had happened before. No doubt the leaders of the sect in southern France added their own peculiar variations to the basic tenets of belief, but those basic tenets were ancient and were shared with others who had lived, almost certainly unknown to the majority of them, in earlier ages and in far-flung places. These basic teachings had always haunted the Christian imagination and in many respects seemed to bear a strong resemblance to what the Church itself professed in its creed and gospel. It was this that gave sects like the Albigensians their special attraction and made them specially dangerous to the Church.

The Albigensians held, as all of their predecessors had held, that two principles ruled in the universe: one good, the other evil. From this basic polarity everything else followed. It was a religion of opposites. From the principle of good had come everything that was spiritual and admirable; from the evil principle had come all that was material and contemptible. Spirit and flesh were incompatible and in a state of perpetual conflict. The world of matter itself was evil, the creation of a malevolent deity. The body, gross and corrupt, imprisoned the soul and was to be treated with scorn; its pleasures were to be subdued by rigorous discipline. A hatred of the flesh was a precondition of salvation. For the elect, evil could be defeated by a suppression of all physical desires in a process of harsh renunciation. For them, the Church, in teaching the doctrine of the resurrection of the body and worshipping God in the Holy Eucharist, had become the instrument of the devil. This radically dualistic interpretation of religion and the universe rejoiced in a vivid mythology of the demonic, and it bequeathed to Western European art, as well as to Christian preaching, some of its iconography of hell and damnation.

Why this type of religion should have arisen in this place at this moment of history is still a matter of much debate. In many ways it seems surprising that so lively, sophisticated and exquisite a civilisation should have been attracted to a religion which apparently hated beauty and condemned all sensual pleasure; unless it could be argued that the most civilised of societies will always be prone to the most morbid of fantasies. That this type of religion did arise should, on the other hand, come as no surprise, for the history of Christianity presents us with a story in which there are irregular but frequent irruptions of dualism. As early as the third century there had occurred a similar challenge to orthodox belief in the form of Manicheism, a powerful variety of dualism which, though denounced by the Church, continued to influence the thinking of many, both inside and outside the Christian community, for several centuries. Augustine of Hippo, one of the most brilliant minds of Christendom, spent a number of years under the influence of Manicheist teachers and, some would argue, never really escaped the pervasive ethos of their doctrines.

Inherent in the human psyche there seems to be an urge to see life in terms of opposites: light and darkness; good and evil; God and the devil. Whether existence does, in fact, fall into binary structures is, of course, questionable, but the fact remains that there has always been an attractiveness in the proposition that every action produces a counter-action; that light could not exist without darkness; that we could not recognise and know the good unless we recognised and knew evil; that the existence of God necessitates the existence of the devil. In this universe of dualistic oppositions the 'problem' of evil can be dealt with in a neat and satisfying way – as the Albigensians, and, before them, the Manichees discovered. Evil is traced back to a single primordial principle of malevolence quite separate from and opposed to God, who is the origin of goodness. The world, of which we are part, is caught up in the supernatural conflict between these warring powers.

While Christianity has always refuted the claims of thorough-going dualism, it has, in its history, consistently painted pictures of and enunciated propositions about the relationship between good and evil that bear a strong similarity to the explanations that dualism offers for the existence of evil. If there really is a supernatural power opposed to God, able to frustrate his will and unravel his designs, God cannot be held to account for the misery of the world. Here is a way out of the dilemmas we have already discussed. The blame for all unhappiness and pain, everything from the Holocaust to headaches, can be laid at the feet of some supernatural force: Satan, the prince of darkness, the devil. A mythology of the devil is present in the Christian religion from the beginning and has to be taken seriously. The great Christian apologist of the late second and early third century, Tertullian, was not a lone voice in professing a belief that the fallen angels, with Satan as their chief, were the ultimate source of all disasters in terrestrial life.[1] He may have expressed his belief with greater vigour than others of his time, but the evidence suggests that most of the Church in the early centuries held to a similar doctrine. What they did not propose, however, was that the conflict between good and evil was endless or that Satan was a force equal to God. They did propose that Christianity was committed, in some way, to a form of dualism within which the question of the existence of evil was to be located. It would have seemed absurd to speak about evil without speaking about the malignancy of extraterrestrial powers.

A modern version of Tertullian's position can be found in a similarly robust Christian apologist, C. S. Lewis. In a broadcast talk of 1942 he delivered this opinion in his customarily forth-right manner:

> Real Christianity (as distinct from Christianity-and-water) goes much nearer to Dualism than people think. One of the things that surprised me when I first read the New Testament seriously was that it was always talking about a Dark Power in the universe – a mighty evil spirit who was held to be behind death and disease, and sin. The difference is that Christianity thinks this Dark Power was created by God, and was good when he was created, and went wrong. Christianity agrees with Dualism that this universe is at war. But it doesn't think this is a war between independent powers. It thinks it's a civil war, a rebellion, and that we are living in a part of the universe occupied by the rebel.[2]

Whether one accepts Lewis' interpretation of Christianity or not, and whether one believes in a devil or not, it is impossible to ignore the supernatural language of the New Testament or fail to see that the vocabulary of Christian literature for nearly two thousand years has been saturated with the imagery of conflict. Did not Jesus Christ himself invoke such a picture of supernatural warfare when he said, 'I saw Satan fall like lightning' (Luke 10:18)?

The writings of the Old Testament, by contrast, are on the whole reticent on the matter of supernatural evil, and it is rarely personified. Satan appears, as we have already seen, in the book of Job and also in the prophecy of Zechariah (chapter 3), but only in the sense of an 'accuser', a servant of the Almighty. The apocalyptic literature of Daniel and Enoch speaks of rebellious angels, and there are some ambiguous references to spiritual powers in the Pentateuch, but the evidence for a full-blooded belief in the existence of hostile supernatural forces is scanty and peripheral. It may be that behind the books which found their way into the canon of the Hebrew Bible there was another, hidden tradition, more sinister and frightening; but it does not surface until much later. The impression given by the canonical books is of a theology which is uncompromisingly monistic. If evil is a reality and has to be recognised as part of the structure of the universe, then God, somehow, is responsible for it:

> I am the Lord, and there is no other;
> besides me there is no god . . .
> I form light and create darkness
> I make weal and create woe
> I am the Lord, who do all these things.

> (Isa. 45:5–7)

It is sometimes easy to forget that this was the soil in which Christianity was planted and, forgetting it, to exaggerate excitedly the dualistic features of the world of the New Testament. Nonetheless, in the kaleidoscopic picture of evil with which we are presented in these writings of the Christian tradition, we cannot fail to be aware of the fact that an acute sense of a non-human, extraterrestrial force has found its way into the Christian imagination. Whether we like it or not, nearly every author seems to believe that the world is in need of deliverance from a power which is alien to it and which has enslaved it against its will. But there is no systematic account of evil, and what is often not clear is what the writers thought about its origin or its nature. Was it personal or impersonal? Could it be named or not? Did it have a beginning, or was it eternal? We are given a number of brilliantly coloured images each of which adds something to the mosaic which the Church inherited from these documents and this period.

Perhaps the closest we come to a systematic theology in the New Testament is in St Paul's epistle to the Romans, and it will be useful to use this carefully controlled piece of writing as a point of entry. The opening chapters lay out, as dispassion-

ately as the apostle can manage, the theological themes that
form the basis of Christian belief. But in chapter 7 the tone
changes and there is wrung from the author's heart the cry of
a man who has not only experienced the joy and fulfilment
of the Christian life, but also its pain and difficulty: 'I can will
what is right, but I cannot do it. For I do not do the good I
want, but the evil I do not want is what I do.' Images of
imprisonment and captivity haunt his imagination: he feels
'occupied' or 'possessed'. 'Now if I do what I do not want, it
is no longer I that do it, but sin that dwells within me', and
'Who will deliver me from this body of death?'

Evil, considered as a theological problem, is not under discussion here. Paul's mind is preoccupied with the notion of sin;
but he has ascribed to sin an objective power such that it has
become personified as *l'autre*, a malignant, false self which
has driven out the real self; or, to change the metaphor, another
Paul has imprisoned the person that Paul is. How does this
other self appear, and whence does it derive its power? He does
not answer that question yet, for the thrust of his thought is
still psychological, the eyes of his mind are still turned inward:
he is puzzling over the experience of the divided self and the
captive spirit.

It is not until he opens out his vision to the cosmos that he
begins to suggest the whence of this appalling power: 'for the
creation was subjected to futility, not of its own will, but by
the will of him who subjected it in hope; because the creation
will be set free from its bondage to decay and obtain the
glorious liberty of the children of God' (Rom. 8:20–22). The
word 'evil' does not appear and the 'him' is not identified, but
the passage makes it clear that iniquity is not reducible to merely
human terms – that is, moral failure which can be corrected
by repentance and amendment of life; it is more mysterious
and more terrible. The images of imprisonment are still present

in the writing, but they have been enriched by suggestions of cosmic warfare and cosmic victory.

Some such notion may lie behind Jesus' famous declaration, 'I saw Satan fall like lightning' (Luke 10:18). We cannot be certain what was in his mind when this statement was made. The context, however, is exorcism, the casting out of demons, and a link between Satan and the demonic is strongly suggested. If Jesus is referring to the legend of a rebel archangel who contended with God and fell from grace, then the Satan mentioned here is a very different creature from the wily character of the story of Job and bears more resemblance to the monstrous pictures of the book of Revelation. The exorcisms performed by Jesus and his followers are thus not only miracles of healing, but victories over evil, and are being placed in a larger framework than the merely natural and human. It is cosmic evil and supernatural conflict which come into view.

Of all the New Testament books, the one which contained the most potent images for the Christian imagination of later ages was the book of the Revelation. Here in lurid colours evil is depicted as a force of immense and terrible power: the angel of the pit, whose name in Hebrew is *Abbadon* and in Greek *Appollyon* (Rev. 9:11), and the dragon which is thrown down from heaven and is called the devil and Satan (Rev. 12:7). Cosmic conflict, the war fought between the angels of light and the angels of darkness, described here in Revelation, became a central image of Christian spirituality and teaching as well as of Christian art and iconography. Given the pictorial vividness of this imagery, it is little wonder that, on the wilder shores of religion, fevered imaginations would try to push the Church into extreme forms of dualism, and that, from time to time, sects like the Manichees and the Albigensians would explode out of the mainstream of Church life and belief to create their own dualistic mythologies using the images drawn from the treasury of biblical writings.

There is no doubt that many contemporary Christians are uneasy with and dismissive of this way of portraying evil. And in our secular era it is difficult to resist the thrust of those who would do away with all forms of dualism and rid the Christian faith of the mythology of cosmic conflict – including the myth of the devil. The books of the New Testament, it is plausibly argued, belong to their peculiar age and culture and must be understood in terms of that age and culture. Our world-view cannot be theirs; their explanation for the existence of evil cannot be ours. In his book *Jesus Christ and Mythology*, Rudolf Bultmann, the most famous of all the 'demythologisers' of the New Testament texts, succinctly summarised the modern difficulty:

> Just as mythological are the presuppositions of the expectation of the Kingdom of God, namely, the theory that the world, although created by God, is ruled by the devil, Satan, and that his army, the demons, is the source of all evil, sin and disease. The whole conception of the world which is presupposed in the teaching of Jesus as in the New Testament generally is mythological; i.e. the conception of the world being structured in three stories, heaven, earth and hell; the conception of the intervention of supernatural powers in the course of events . . . This conception of the world we call mythological because it is different from the conception of the world which has been formed and developed by modern science . . .[3]

According to this view we can no longer believe in the universe of the New Testament and so treat evil as though it were an objective, supernatural force – for belief in a supernatural world has itself become questionable. There is no real conflict between the powers of light and darkness, good and evil. We are left to deal with the images as best we can from our own scientific, secularised standpoint. These pictures from the past may be useful as symbolic representations of an essentially subjective, psychological and emotional state, but that is all they can be. Religion has been radically interiorised: in a world dominated by science, by what can be observed and precisely calculated, religion becomes less a matter of faith in the super-natural and worship of the Divine than a matter of moral choice and authentic existence. Not only can the image of the devil be exorcised, but the concept of God can be dissolved into the vocabulary of self-aspiration, self-fulfilment and self-transcendence.

Perhaps this the end of the story: it might be argued that the long history of the Christian mind trying to imagine evil shows an inevitable evolutionary progress towards this end. But before we close the page on dualism we need to take note of a situation that sits uncomfortably with this reading of the story. One of the most surprising features of modern, technological society is the persistence of belief, among sections of society which have no attachment to any specifically religious community, in the existence of evil as some kind of objective external force: a yearning for the dualistic interpretation of the universe. More-over, we have witnessed, in the last thirty years, an astonishing growth of Evangelical Christianity – much of it fundamentalist in character – in all parts of the world. The vast majority of those who are members of these groups hold beliefs about evil and the devil that are far closer to the views of C. S. Lewis than those of Rudolf Bultmann. It is not easy to explain this phenomenon, just as it is not easy to explain the phenomenon of the tenacity, at the level of popular culture, of the vocabulary and imagery of dualism. It comes as a shock to those of us who believe ours is a profoundly secular society to discover that exorcism of one kind or another is still practised in many Christian communities and that Satanism, as a cult, is still taken seriously. The devil, in one guise after another, still seems to exercise a fascination over the popular imagination. One would have assumed that in this sceptical and enlightened age evil could never be regarded as anything other than the perverted disposition of the human heart and will and that the idea of the demonic belonged only in the realm of childish fancy. No doubt much of the 'imaginings' of evil does not rise above the level of childish fancy, but its prevalence has still to be accounted for. No serious study has yet been made of dualistic imagery in popular culture (films, books, music), so one cannot yet say what this signifies; but it cannot be ignored. At this stage all one can say is that the kind of anti-supernatural, ethical religion typical of Enlightenment culture and the modern demytholo-gisers is about as remote from popular culture as can be. It seems, as Peter Vardy has recently remarked, 'there is something deep in the human psyche which accepts the reality of these forces'.[4]

# 4

## DOES A SHADOW
## EXIST?

'To MEET THE unequalled strains and excitement of the age
he brought an unequalled power. That power he derived from
Africa, that stony yet not unfertile land, which engendered
tremendous crops, tremendous men, violent events.' The words
are those of Rebecca West and the man she is describing is a
fourth-century Christian, St Augustine of Hippo (354–430).[1]
That this clear-sighted, erudite and sceptical woman seems to
have been captivated by her subject and wrote one of the most
psychologically acute biographical studies of him should not,
perhaps, come as a surprise. She was always fascinated by enig-
matic personalities and the exercise of power in complex and
turbulent societies. In Augustine she found a profoundly paradoxical character living at one of those moments in history
which sees the 'shift' of civilised sensibility: the end of the
Roman empire and the classical age and the beginning, in
confusion and uncertainty, of Christian Europe. The personality
and theology of Augustine was to mould the new civilisation
which was struggling to be born out of the old. His genius
towers over the centuries that followed, directing the intellectual
and spiritual life of the society that was being created, shaping
its church and politics, and bequeathing to theology a theory
of evil which is as subtle, complicated and paradoxical as his
own personality. His whole life revolved around the concept

34

and practice of love: seldom has love been so passionately and tenderly described. Yet, while pouring out his soul in ecstasies of love, he seems to have been preoccupied with the horrors of sin and the possibilities of damnation. He judged the human condition with a harshness and ferocity that is barely tolerable to modern ears, yet he resolutely refused to define evil as anything but 'the absence of good'.

Rebecca West uses a peculiar term when trying to convey to her readers his huge, untidy, authoritative achievement: she calls it 'romantic'.

> Though that system is not entirely satisfactory, though it abounds in false assumptions and contradictions, it still remains one of the most stupendous works of man. Augustine's errors were the result of his position in time and so are not disgraceful. It was for him to be the great romantic artist, leaning far out to the apprehension of yet unformulated truths, and bringing in the false mingled with the true in an immense mass of material which was reduced to order by the great classical artist, St Thomas Aquinas. We have here one of the first and most impressive demonstrations that all classicism depends upon a previous romanticism.[2]

One may dispute her conclusion, but one can recognise the appropriateness of her description. There is, in Augustine, that restlessness and energy which we nowadays associate with the romantic spirit, a certain intellectual and emotional recklessness, an attempt to express the inexpressible and break through to some new experience, an ability to live with contradictions and celebrate paradox. It was, as Rebecca West says, left to later ages (and particularly to Thomas Aquinas) to try to perceive the order in, or impose the order on, this intractable material, not least on Augustine's writings on the subject of evil.

The story of Augustine on evil, and the answer to our question 'Does a shadow exist?' begins with dualism; that is, with the Manicheism to which he was drawn as a young man in Carthage. This philosophical system, so attractive in its apparent simplicity, seemed to answer the problem with which he was already becoming obsessed: the problem of evil and sin, both in himself and in the whole world around him. Augustine tells the story of his encounter with, attraction to, and eventual disillusionment with Manicheism in his *Confessions*, that intriguing work of autobiography which serves as a highly wrought key to the understanding of his mind and his theology. It is not difficult to see why a young man full of passion, both intellectual and sensual, should have been drawn towards the Manichean system, with its dramatic opposition of good and evil and its stern demands upon its followers to live a life of moral rigour. The cool, detached, 'unsensual' personality has never found dualistic systems attractive: it is the sensualist who is drawn to the extremes of the dualistic universe and the renunciation of the flesh. Augustine had passion and imagination in abundance and was easy prey.

Looking back on his years as a Manichee, he wrote of his growing unease. After nine or perhaps ten years he seems to have reached a point of crisis and eagerly awaited the visit to Carthage of a famous Manichean teacher, Faustus. The meeting was not a success. Augustine discovered that the celebrated orator, though eloquent and graceful in his utterance, was not as well educated as he was and was unconvincing in philosophical discussion: 'After he had clearly showed his lack of training in liberal arts in which I had supposed him to be highly qualified, I began to lose all hope that he would be able to analyse and resolve the difficulties which disturbed me.'[3]

At the centre of those 'difficulties' was, of course, the problem of evil. Manicheism, with its theories of cosmic conflict, of good and evil locked in eternal combat, had enabled the young man, up to this point in his life, to find a solution to the bewildering sense of his own divided self. It suggested that he was not responsible for the greed and lust of his own existence, and that human beings were not the cause, ultimately, of the wickedness of society, because the origin of evil lay elsewhere, in a cosmic force. But the solution did not prove satisfying to the troubled and inquiring spirit of Augustine. The Manichean contempt for the material world distressed a man whose delight in the beauty of Nature was an ineradicable part of his being; and the farrago of myths which festooned the central tenets of Manichean doctrine seemed to him to be absurd.

Manicheism was abandoned, and for a while it seemed that the sophisticated abstractions of Neoplatonism would help him to understand and resolve the difficulties which disturbed him. For centuries Christians had been drawing upon the philosophical vocabulary of Neoplatonism to illuminate the truths of the faith, and it was natural that Augustine would look to this most pervasive of philosophical systems for an answer to his problems. Furthermore, it is easy to see why Neoplatonism should be the most obvious step for a man who has just abandoned Manicheism to take. There is not the same dualism in Neoplatonism as there is in Manicheism, but there is, nonetheless, a rejection of the material world in favour of a spiritual one. Gone are the imagery of cosmic conflict and the bizarre myths: in their place is a highly rational system of thought and a discipline of abstraction. The soul must learn how to abstract itself from the body by way of intellectual apprehension; the self must acquire the art of abstraction from all sensual experience so that intellectual union with the Absolute can be achieved. The human soul was seen in most Neoplatonic systems as a fallen being caught temporarily in the cage of matter, the body, from which it must escape and rise by means of intellectual endeavour to the contemplation of the Supreme Being. This Being was not, of course, to be confused with the Judaeo-Christian God of love, mercy and compassion, but was Pure Being beyond the

reach of earthbound description. G. R. Evans summarises
the teaching of the Neoplatonist teacher Porphyry:

> Once, before the Fall, we were intellectual beings; we were still
> rational, but our reason is impeded from its proper operation by
> the senses. It follows . . . that we must try to return to our
> former condition by living in the intellect, and not through
> our bodily senses; and 'conjuction' with things allied to the
> body (such as thinking in 'bodily images') is false.[4]

That stress on 'the intellect' was central to the whole system
of Neoplatonism. It was an emphasis that would colour everything Augustine did and wrote: it entered his religious sensibility
and remained embedded there throughout his life. It became
part of the puzzle and the tragedy of the saint, and entered the
bloodstream of Western Christianity to create both glory and
shame. He whose characteristic mode of existence was via the
senses deliberately chose a philosophy which denied the validity
of sensual experience: a man whose natural mode of self-
expression and communication was via the vividness of 'bodily
imagery' deliberately embraced a religious vocabulary which
refused to acknowledge that Divinity could be apprehended by
anything but abstract concepts. Perhaps, if Augustine had been
a less generous and passionate man, he might have remained a
Neoplatonist, for he seems to have been enthralled by this
philosophy. But he was by temperament a lover of things and
people and Nature, and this longing to give and receive love
by means of the senses could never be satisfied by a philosophy
like this, however mystically it might express itself. As Rebecca
West remarks: 'This delicate Neoplatonism had no real chance
of holding Augustine whose most severely abstract thought is
damp with his sweat.'[5]

We shall find that when it comes to the question of evil she
is right: here Augustine is often at his most severely abstract,
yet here, at the same time, all his imaginings of evil are drenched

with the sweat of his personal struggle. In Milan, under the guidance of the great bishop Ambrose, Augustine left Neoplatonism for Christianity; but not before he had gathered to himself, as I have already indicated, certain aspects of that teaching which could never be erased from his thought. One of these was a conception of evil as a kind of nihilism; not a cosmic principle at war with goodness, but a nothingness, 'something' which had fallen away from being.

In the seventh book of the *Confessions* Augustine gives us an account of his search for the answer to the problem of evil in a reconstruction of the movement of his thoughts from the perspective of faith:

> ... where and whence is evil? How did it creep in? What is its root and what is its seed? Or does it not have any being? Why should we fear and avoid what has no being? If our fear is vain, it is certain that fear itself is evil, and that the heart is groundlessly disturbed and tortured ... Where then does it come from since the good God made everything good? ... Is it that the matter from which he made things was somehow evil?

Augustine rejected the Manichean solution that matter could, in itself, be evil; instead he adopted, from the Neoplatonists, the doctrine that evil could never be considered to be 'substantial', but was a lack, an absence. It could have no real, independent existence; it was not the opposite of good, but the absence of good, a 'nothing' a *privatio boni*. As a Christian Augustine was committed to the assertion that everything that God had created was good, and since God was the Creator of everything, evil could have no real existence, for this would be to suppose another creator. Evil was the absence of good in the same way that sickness was the absence of health and darkness was the absence of light. Does a shadow exist? Not of itself. It is defined by the light which does exist: it comes into 'being' and can be observed and experienced only as a result of the withdrawal of the light. The seductive propositions of dualism were that everything can be known by its direct and complementary opposite; that the structure of reality is binary and our knowledge of the world is essentially bi-focal. This theory, which makes good and evil totally interdependent, Augustine set aside for a more abstract, subtle theory.

Years after the *Confessions* Augustine summarised his beliefs in his small compendium of Christian teaching, the *Enchiridion*:

> What, after all, is anything we call evil but the privation of good? In animal bodies, for instance, sickness and wounds are nothing but the privation of health. When a cure is effected, the evils which were present (i.e. the sickness and the wounds) do not retreat and go elsewhere, they simply do not exist any more. For such evil is not a substance; the wound or the disease is a defect of the bodily substance which, as a Substance, is good. Evil, then, is called an accident, i.e. a privation of that good which is called health.

In this way Augustine solved two troubling problems. First, if evil did not 'exist', God could not be held responsible for it. Secondly, by calling it the absence of good, the sovereignty of the Almighty in the universe was preserved: there could be no other Principle or Being that was creating structures and situations beyond his power. But while it solved some problems it created others.

It may have entered the intellect of Western theology as the most plausible explanation of evil, but it failed to capture the Christian imagination: it seemed preposterously abstract to those who did not live their lives at the level of philosophical abstraction. And, it has to be admitted, Augustine's Neoplatonic vocabulary fitted awkwardly with much of the traditional Christian teaching about evil. 'Do you renounce the devil and all his works?' asks the interrogator at the rite of Baptism. And those about to be baptised answer: 'We do.' But who, then, is this devil, and where are his works? If evil is only an absence, it cannot be imagined and certainly cannot be personified.

If Christianity were nothing more than a philosophical system, a collection of abstract speculations, the theory of evil as *privatio boni* would be perfectly acceptable. It would not have to be imagined – and we have seen how dangerously close Augustine came to wanting to free Christianity from 'bodily imaginings'. Here the Neoplatonic influence is at its most insidious. But this is not the way in which a religion (except, possibly, Buddhism) works. Religion captures the whole of life, it articulates the new life in prayer and worship, movement and ritual, story and prophecy. The imagination will play at least as large a part as the intellect. Even Islam, that way of life most wary of idolatry and most severe in its condemnation of the making of images, has a holy book replete with sensuous imagery, including, of course, images of evil vividly presented.

So it is with Christianity. Despite the fact that, at the level of theological discourse, Augustine's account of the nature of evil was received into the tradition and became widely accepted as orthodox belief, depictions of evil in thousands of guises appeared everywhere: in illuminated manuscripts and carvings; on the walls of churches; in the movements of the liturgy; in sermons and meditations and poetry. The dualism which Augustine had so deliberately and ingeniously avoided burst out in a multitude of images in the centuries that followed. It would need more than the brilliance of Augustine's theology to eradicate the experience of evil as a reality. Evil was felt as fact, something known and feared. How, it was implicitly asked in the hundreds of thousands of pictures that surrounded ordinary lives and expressed ordinary reactions, could one have an experience of something that did not exist? The closing petition of the Lord's Prayer sounded unnecessary, or at least melodramatic, when evil was interpreted in this way. Was one praying to be delivered from nothing? No, whatever Augustine may have said, as far as the vast majority of ordinary Christians were concerned, evil existed and could be portrayed in words and pictures: the fight against it was real, the prayers about deliverance from it were genuine and fervent.

But perhaps this account of Augustine's theory of evil is inadequate. How could a man who so clearly felt the misery as well as the splendour of life leave his explanation of the problem of evil at the level of the Neoplatonist philosophy? The answer is: he could not and did not. 'In Augustine's Christianity, the sense of sin is the narrow gate through which all must pass who would see the truth . . . No one can say "Evil be thou my good"; the lie that every man utters in the moment of sin is that evil is his good.'[6] He returned to the problem over and over again in sermons, treatises, letters and commentaries, trying to construct a theory that was not only comprehensive and intelligible, but true to experience and faith. He ran into almost insurmountable difficulties. How was one to deal with the notion of cosmic evil? Like almost everyone of his age, he accepted without question the existence of the devil and the legions of fallen angels. He held firmly to the belief that Christ's death and resurrection was the victory over sin and the deliverance from the power of supernatural evil. But he remained disconcertingly vague on the difficult question of why angelic beings should have turned away from goodness and light and plunged into darkness and rebellion, and why they should have the power to imprison the hearts and minds of men and women. He often spoke of demonic creatures as though they were objective forces of evil, but failed, satisfactorily, to explain how a 'no-thing' could be a force. Above all, there was the question of Satan. According to his theory, evil was ultimately self-defeating and could accomplish nothing; a totally evil being could not exist, by definition. The arguments went round and round and in and out. Was Satan, perhaps, to be regarded as having retained in himself some elements of goodness, even in his fallenness? Could he, therefore, be redeemed – as one of Augustine's great predecessors, Origen, had argued? This he denied.[7] On and on he went, searching for answers.

The fact that Augustine's theory was both enormously influential and yet felt by many to be paradoxical to the point of self-contradiction can be illustrated by a story recounted by G. R. Evans in her book, *Augustine on Evil*:

> In the monastery at Bec in northern France in the late eleventh century, St Anselm's pupils used to ask him why, if evil is nothing, it matters whether or not we sin, for it would seem that sin is nothing: 'If sin is nothing,' they said, 'why does God punish man for sin, for no-one ought to be punished for nothing.'[8]

We may smell a whiff of the scholastic mind in this teasing question: always ready to press an argument, logically, to a conclusion, however absurd. But we may also have some sympathy with it, for the concept of evil as privation, absence or lack conveys a frustrating sense of abstraction: the atmosphere of the philosopher's study, remote from the experience of the violence, cruelty and hatred of the real world. Augustine, who had suffered the pains of the real world and knew it better than most, knew that perfectly well and had more to say on the subject.

For more than a decade after the sack of the imperial city of Rome by the Visigoths in 410 Augustine laboured on his extraordinary work, *The City of God*. In Book XI he addresses the problem of evil again, but not before he has considered the nature of creation:

> For leaving aside the utterances of the prophets, we have the evidence of the world itself in all its ordered change and movement and in all the beauty it presents to our sight, a world

43

which bears a kind of silent testimony to the fact of its creation, and proclaims that its maker could have been none other than God, the ineffably and invisibly great, the ineffably and invisibly beautiful.[9]

The clue we are looking for is to be found in the words 'ordered change and movement'. If evil is defined as *privatio* or absence, we may ask: an absence of what? The answer comes back, 'good', *privatio boni*. Is this sufficient explanation? In what does this goodness consist, and how should we recognise it? Augustine answers in terms of order: of things being in a right relation to one another. Without order there would be chaos and we could know nothing; without order there could be no unity, for it is only in a proper ordering that disparate things may be united without confusion or destruction. Order is the characteristic of the work and love of God, of creation and redemption. Disorder is the sign of sin: evil is the privation, the absence, of order. Over and over again he prays that the disordered wills of human beings may be so governed by the Spirit of God that they will be reordered and given that which they lack, and were deprived of, before. His view of the original creation was of a glorious ordering of the constituent parts of the universe; his view of fallen creation was, conversely, a view of the disruption of that order. Each human being is evil – that is, disordered: the appetites at war with the intellect; the bodily parts at war with themselves, resulting in disfigurement and disease. Human society – the city – is disordered: men and women in conflict out of greed, envy or lust. The order of the heavenly hierarchy had been disrupted by the rebellion of Satan.

And so the Devil did not stand firm in the truth, and yet he did not escape the judgement of the truth. He did not continue in the tranquility of order; but that did not mean he escaped from the power of the imposer of order.[10]

44

There is an order to be known, loved and accepted. Disordered love is love of the lesser instead of the greater; the preference of the lower to the higher; resting content with earthly delights; being satisfied with the beauty of this world instead of the beauty of God. (This puts into perspective Augustine's ambivalent attitude to 'bodily images'.) The absence of order – the attempted perversion of what *is* – can be felt and depicted even while, paradoxically, we can say that it is an absence. To attempt to embrace the impossible and make it real is to say 'Evil be thou my good' and to try to make it so. But because evil has no real being, one wills oneself out of existence: hell is populated with those who have tried to live by illusion, by a lie, by pretending that nothing is something.

Twelve hundred years after Augustine a character in a great epic poem was to utter those precise words and make them his creed. Did John Milton in *Paradise Lost* understand what Augustine had meant? There was one who did understand what Augustine meant and depicted it in an unforgettable way: Dante Alighieri in *The Divine Comedy*.

# MEDIEVAL
# TRANSFORMATIONS

IN HIS BOOK on the literature of courtly love, *The Allegory of Love*, C. S. Lewis neatly points up the way in which the modern European mind has oscillated between contrarities in its estimation of the society and culture of the Middle Ages, and especially of the religion of that era. 'From some accounts we should conclude that medieval Christianity was a kind of Manicheism seasoned with prurience: from others that it was a sort of carnival in which the happier aspects of Paganism took part, after being baptized and yet losing none of their jollity.'[1] It would still be true to say that, apart from those who have a special interest in the medieval world, the word 'medieval' itself is used, popularly, more often as a term of abuse rather than as one of approbation. It has become a synonym of all that is unenlightened, obscurantist and superstitious. No doubt there was much about life in the Middle Ages that was, even by its own standards, all of those things, but even the most superficial examination of the history of the era will reveal the glories of its art and architecture, the nobility of its many ideals, the power and coherence of its intellectual achievements and the depths of its piety.

One of the aspects of medieval life that the modern mind finds most difficult to comprehend, and one it almost automatically condemns, is its thoroughgoing 'supernaturalism'. It was, for the most part, a society in which it was universally accepted that the natural world of physical reality and everyday occurrences was interpenetrated by a supernatural world of spiritual forces. The natural and supernatural worlds collided with one another and explained one another. A human being was a citizen of two cities: the one that could be seen and the one that, except in peculiar circumstances, could not. The whole arena of natural events, moreover, could be interpreted as a complex system of signs which indicated the nature of supernatural existence. A person's day-to-day actions, however small and apparently insignificant, were linked to supernatural ends. One was surrounded by unseen presences and in touch with unseen forces that were both terrifying and transforming in their power. It is this aspect of life, this assumption of the coinherence of the natural and supernatural, that gives the medieval imaginings of evil their distinctive quality and shape. In many ways they appear to us as dramatically dualistic and a far cry from the sophisticated theories of Augustine. The distinguished medieval scholar Jacques Le Goff renders the picture as follows:

He [man] was the prize in a contest that often surpassed him, the struggle of Satan, the spirit of evil, against God and against good. Christianity had, of course, rejected and condemned Manicheism . . . There was but one God, a God of goodness . . . who was superior to Satan . . . but who has nevertheless left Satan extensive powers over man . . . Man's salvation or damnation was the stakes in a battle between supernatural armies of demons and angels . . . Man's soul was also portrayed in the Middle Ages as a miniature person being weighed by St. Michael in the scales of judgement, under the watchful eye of Satan, who waits for a chance to tip the beam to his side, and St. Peter poised to intervene on the side of the good.[2]

This is, probably, too simple an account of the religious

sensibility of any period of European society in the Middle Ages, but there is a good deal of evidence, especially from the plastic arts of painting and sculpture, to back up the contention that for much of the era and for a large part of the population the picture is, on the whole and in its broad lines, accurate. The radical dualism of good and evil, which Augustine was so intent upon eliminating from Christian philosophy and practice, still haunted the Christian imagination and was everywhere to be observed – most obviously and dramatically in the tympana over the great doors of Romanesque and Gothic cathedrals which greeted worshippers as they made their way into the buildings. Whatever the fine minds of Christian scholars might think, and however they might try to explain it away, the people believed in the existence of evil and its power in their lives. In the middle of the thirteenth century we find canon law being promulgated to deal with witchcraft, and in doing so treating evil as a positive and fearsome force:

> Bishops and their officials must labour with all their strength to uproot thoroughly from their parishes the pernicious art of sorcery and malefice invented by the Devil. For the Apostle says, 'A man that is a heretic after the first and second admonition avoid.' Those are held captive by the Devil who, leaving their creator, seek the aid of the Devil.[3]

In all this we may see the elaboration of what was there in Christianity from the beginning. The Church of the Middle Ages saw itself as continuing the practice and tradition received from an earlier age. The point has been made many times by many scholars that the demarcations of history – the Classical Era, the Dark Ages, the Middle Ages – are of limited usefulness and can be, frequently, misleading. It is obvious that the men and women of the twelfth or thirteenth century did not think of their time as a 'middle age'. (Whether or not they thought of themselves as 'modern' is another matter: modernity is itself a 'modern' concept.) What they did believe was that their age was a direct continuation of an age which preceded it, and in this continuity they believed that they accepted and held to the traditions and attitudes of previous generations. They seldom saw themselves as innovators; originality was not prized, and the Church was, in the main, a conservative force. What they could not see was the extent to which they were original and actually transformed ideas from the past. Nor did they have much sense of that which seems clear to us: the parallel, sometimes conflicting, interpretations of spiritual and theological traditions running throughout their lives.

The perception of evil offers us one of the clearest examples of these counterpointing interpretations. The Church had not only received a modified dualism from the past, it had also received the writings of the most influential figure of Christian history since the biblical authors: Augustine. Along with the depictions of evil as a supernatural force in art, architecture and preaching went the theology of evil that seemed to contradict that dualism: evil as 'no-thing', *privatio boni*. And wrestling with these contradictions were two of the formative influences of Western European culture: Thomas Aquinas and Dante Alighieri. They were as important in their own ways as Augustine was in his in their shaping of Christian sensibility. William Neil writes:

> If the seminal works of the Dark Ages may be said to be St Jerome's *Vulgate* and St Augustine's *City of God*, the correspondingly significant literary milestones in the Middle Ages are St Thomas Aquinas' *Summa Theologica* and the *Divine Comedy* of Dante Alighieri. This was not only the greatest of his works, and indeed one of the greatest literary masterpieces of all time, it embodied the medieval mind.[4]

To those who are interested in the growth and development of Christian doctrine, Thomas' reception and transmission of the Augustinian theology which he had inherited is one of the most intriguing facets of his huge achievement. While he consistently acknowledged Augustine as a revered and undisputed master in spiritual and theological matters, he just as consistently reinterpreted him, altering emphases, exploiting ambiguities, juxtaposing the fourth-century saint's assertions with those of quite different thinkers such as Aristotle, Boethius or Dionysius; extrapolating from Augustine's text to reach his own conclusions; subtly reading the mind of the earlier scholar through the lens of his own age and his own very different sensibility. We recall Rebecca West's comments on the 'romanticism' of Augustine and the 'classicism' of Thomas. The majestic rationality of Thomas Aquinas received the tempestuous outpourings of Augustine imperturbably, and calmly set about the task of channelling them into a vast, coherent theological system without impairing their profundity or contradicting their validity. No two men could have been more unlike one another in temperament: almost every word that Augustine wrote was in some way or other autobiographical, words drawn out by the passion of an immediate concern. Almost every sentence of Thomas conveys, by contrast, a heart and soul at peace and a mind serenely contemplating the mysteries of the universe with a kind of joyful detachment.

The quality of this difference between the two men is brilliantly illuminated by their approaches to the problem of evil. Augustine circled around it restlessly, trying to uncover and grasp its dark heart: Thomas deals with it on his way to the exposition of, for him, grander themes. In the enormous spaces of the *Summa Theologica*, for instance, the problem of evil occupies only a small corner. It is not that he regarded the problem as trivial, but at the level of theological discourse it was not as central to his concerns as it was to Augustine's. It was a question of proportion. That sense of the anguish of life, of loss, bafflement and despair which drove Augustine's theology was foreign to Thomas.

Existential panic, which has, so often, led to an acute awareness of evil, was not part of his temperament. So his treatment of the problem and the particular place he assigned to it in his theological system comes to us with a quite different air.

All that having been said, it comes as no surprise that he embraces Augustine's concept of evil as negation whole-heartedly. Repeating the essential affirmation of his predecessor, he asserts firmly that evil can only be described as the absence of good; it can have no real, independent existence:

In fact, evil is simply a privation of something which a subject is entitled by its origin to possess and which it ought to have, as we have said. Such is the meaning of the word 'evil' among all men. Now, privation is not an essence; it is, rather, a negation in a substance.

Now, what is evil in itself cannot be natural to anything. For it is of the very definition of evil that it be a privation of that which is to be in a subject by virtue of its natural origin, and which should be in it. So, evil cannot be natural to any subject, since it is a privation of what is natural. Consequently, whatever is present naturally in something is good for it, and is evil if the thing lacks it.[5]

It can have no formal cause since it is not form but lack of form; and it can 'achieve' nothing since it lacks the order necessary for attainment of a goal. This interpretation is rooted in Thomas' understanding of the nature of God. Even more emphatically than Augustine, and certainly more consistently, Thomas identifies goodness with being. The primary description of God in Thomas' writings is *He Who Is*. God is Being: nothing else has being or can come into being apart from God, who is the cause of all being. There is no principle of causation, natural or supernatural, other than God. God cannot create evil because it is logically impossible to conceive of such a condition.

Evil cannot be created, as it is an absence, not a presence; a lack of being, not a peculiar kind of being.

Such an approach and such a definition, as we have seen in the case of Augustine, seems immediately offensive to the modern mind. There appears to be a failure here to come to grips with the realities of experience; a failure, perhaps of the imagination. This abstract language of negation, so neat and logically coherent, does not seem to mesh with the horrors of real life, in which a tiny child can die agonisingly of a disease (see *The Plague*) and millions are slaughtered in Hitler's concentration camps. In such occurrences as these evil is experienced as a reality, as something which is obscene and terrifyingly *there*.

But, just as there was more to be said for Augustine, so there is more to be said about the thought of Thomas, and for much the same reason; though it must be admitted that the rational, detached, scholastic manner of Thomas' presentation has always led (with some justification) to the accusation that his theology was primarily philosophical speculation rather than an attempt to wrestle with the real problems of faith and experience. But, in the end, I think the accusation is unfair, for his world-view is not, essentially, a clever exposition of a synthetic optimism which lacks the courage to face the terrors of life. It is rooted in a doctrine of the invincible providence of God and a concept of an ordered universe. Having firmly declared in the 49th Question of the *Summa Theologica* that 'evil is the absence of the good' and the 'privation of form', he goes on to say that this absence must be understood as the absence of 'order': 'neither has it a final cause, but rather is it a privation of order to the proper end; for not only the end has the nature of good, but also the useful, which is ordered to the end.'[6] Here is Thomas transforming Augustine again: adapting the Augustinian notion of order by way of Aristotle, a philosopher virtually unknown to Augustine, and by way of Aristotle's concept of 'entelechy', which he, Thomas, in turn, puts to wholly Christian use. The key phrase is 'order to the proper end'. Thomas is the great theologian of order, but this order is never a static concept: the universe is ordered to an end and purpose and is moving towards that end under the benign providence of a loving God. Human beings are destined to arrive at the end of their desires and achieve the purpose for which they were created: the beatific vision. As in the thought of Augustine, evil is seen as the absence of order, not simply nothing, naked absence; and absence cannot be known or experienced of itself – it is always the absence of something already existing, and that something is order. Each individuality, according to Thomas, exists not only in itself and for itself but also for other individualities: it possesses its own being only in relation to theirs and cannot know itself or achieve its purpose except in the relation for which it was created. When the proper order in the relation of one thing to another is disrupted the resulting chaos is seen as evil. There is what he called a 'privation of form'. What ought to be there is not there and what is not there is order. The result is not just emptiness, incompleteness or inanition, but disfigurement and distortion, and it can be terrible in its consequences. Disorder can produce the disease from which little children suffer and die in the fictional city of Oran as well as the persecution of the Jews by the Nazis in Hitler's Germany. The disordered state of the universe, furthermore, allows for the possibility of hell and damnation. Those beings, angelic or human, who are wilfully and obstinately disordered make for themselves their condition of perdition. They have lost that for which they were created and were intended to enjoy.

To the troubling question of why the disordered state should have arisen at all in a universe which was originally created in goodness and harmony, Thomas provides answers which may not satisfy the modern mind. These answers rest upon his belief that God's creation is of a world in which all spiritual beings, angels as well as humans, are free: free to respond to or turn away from the love that has called them into being. Acceptance of this grace enables them to achieve the potentiality inherent in their natures. Rejection is the rejection of their own capacities, and from this all moral evil arises: greed, oppression, cruelty and so on. It is not possible, Thomas argues, for God to have created a world in which human beings can make real, free choices and at the same time make sure that the way of rejection and negation is never chosen.

It is a nice point whether, on these grounds, God can logically be held to be responsible for evil. Thomas argues that this does not follow, but if God created a world in which such radical freedom and genuine choice exists, then he at least allows for the possibility of evil being generated and continued. It is easy to see how moral evil like injustice and cruelty can be traced back to the 'disordered wills and affections of sinful men', but what of the problem with which we began: the child dying in agony from an incurable disease? Here the answer is even less satisfying – inevitably, for the problem is more perplexing. Thomas places the discussion of natural disaster in the context, again, of the doctrine of Providence; and in reply to the question of innocent suffering he answers that, if we could see the world from the perspective of the loving Creator, we should see that all happenings, even the most horrible and painful, are directed towards the end of achieving only what is good. There is a memorable phrase in Boethius' *Consolations of Philosophy* which perhaps Thomas knew but does not quote: 'All Fortune is Good Fortune.'

But such an answer is cold comfort to those enduring the terrible pains of torture or violent loss. We saw Camus' rejection of this position in the character of Dr Rieux. When asked to love what he could not understand, he replied, 'I've a very different idea of love. And until my dying day I shall refuse to love a scheme of things in which children are put to torture.'

Is this arrogance? The book of Job has suggested that it is. It is impossible for us to 'see things from God's perspective' except through the eyes of faith, and faith is often severely shaken in the face of extreme pain and innocent suffering. The humble submission of Job, 'I despise myself and repent in dust and ashes', seems, tragically, beyond the reach of millions who have been twisted into anger and bitterness by the apparently senseless sufferings they have endured or witnessed.

Thomas Aquinas, for all his intellectual power and personal sanctity, frequently fails to engage with our modern sensibility. This might be our fault as much as it is his: we are unaccustomed to the relentlessly rational dissection of existential problems by the scholastic mind; the apparent removal of heart-rending experience from the sphere of felt life to the regions of speculative inquiry. We ask for something more because we are used to something different. There was born nine years before Thomas died a man who would give something more, who would have the capacity to unite feeling and intellect, who would be able to take Thomas' theological propositions and turn them into poetry: this man was Dante Alighieri. He 'imagined' evil as profoundly as anyone who has ever lived. Of course, this is not all he did, and his finest achievement, *The Divine Comedy*, written in the opening decades of the fourteenth century, is not simply the theology of Thomas Aquinas put into verse. But the great theologian occupied a central place in Dante's thought, and Thomas' elucidation of the problem of evil is transformed by the imagination of Dante into poetry which enables the heart as well as the mind to apprehend the truths that Thomas was reaching for.

As Thomas was the theologian of order, so Dante became the poet of order: the very shape of *The Divine Comedy* exemplifies this. It is controlled by the number three, the numerical sign of the Holy Trinity. The medieval mind delighted in the symbolic possibilities of number, and Dante exploits these possibilities to the utmost. There are three sections *Inferno*, *Purgatorio* and *Paradiso*. *Purgatorio* and *Paradiso* each comprise 33 cantos; *Inferno* has 34 (i.e. 33 plus a prologue); all these add up to a perfect number, 100. The entire structure rests upon an invariable rhyme scheme, the *terza rima*, in which every alternate line rhymes – through thousands of lines of poetry. The effect astonishes, and sometimes dismays, the modern reader; but the complex outward organisation of the poem is not merely the display of a prodigious literary talent, it is the immediately observable indication of the intellectual preoccupation of the author. What is presented, throughout the poem, is a concrete demonstration of the significance of order. The whole poem, in its very construction, acts as a metaphor of order. The theological point being made by this symbolic means is that the universe – everything from the seraphim and cherubim to rocks and trees – is created to exist in a glorious and harmonious hierarchy which is held together by the love of its creator. And love, as Dante makes clear, is the force which accomplishes this feat: like gravity, it is the law of the universe. It is as foolish to pretend that there is another law by which we can live as it is to pretend that we can flout the law of gravity. If we step into space we shall fall: if we refuse to love we shall die. In *The Divine Comedy* there is a kind of literal fall – into hell. Sin is seen as the deliberate attempt to disrupt this order, the wilful refusal to acknowledge that this 'ordering' of life is the only reality there is. Either it or its absence has to be known, for there is no other reality to know. Evil, as in the theology of both Augustine and Thomas, resides in the absence of order, the perversion of the fact of being.

In the poem Dante, at first in the company of the Roman poet Virgil, later in the company of his beloved Beatrice, makes the journey from a state of bewilderment and fear through the regions of hell, then through purgatory to paradise and the beatific vision:

Midway in the journey of our life I found myself in a dark wood, for the straight way was lost. Ah, how hard it is to tell what that wood was, wild, rugged, harsh; the very thought of it renews the fear! It is so bitter that death is hardly more so.[7]

The first stage of the journey takes the pilgrim (Dante) through hell, the world of the damned, the lost souls, *la perduta gente*. Before Dante and Virgil enter this place of misery and horror they must pass through the gate over which is inscribed words that have become some of the most famous in the literature of Western Europe. 'Abandon all hope you who enter here.' But this line, so well known to millions who have never read the *Comedy*, is part of a longer admonition and description known only to those who have read it. It encapsulates the essence of Dante's Christian faith:

> THROUGH ME YOU ENTER THE WOEFUL CITY,
> THROUGH ME YOU ENTER ETERNAL GRIEF,
> THROUGH ME YOU ENTER AMONG THE LOST.
> JUSTICE MOVED MY HIGHER MAKER:
> THE DIVINE POWER MADE ME,
> THE SUPREME WISDOM, AND THE PRIMAL LOVE.
> BEFORE ME NOTHING WAS CREATED
> IF NOT ETERNAL, AND ETERNAL I ENDURE.
> ABANDON EVERY HOPE, YOU WHO ENTER.[8]

So dreadful are the words that, on first hearing them, we, like the pilgrim in the story, recoil in disbelief. Can this really be the Christian God he is speaking about? Can this really be a picture of the Christian universe? It is only when one begins to scrutinise the text and elucidate the meaning of the theology that one begins to realise the profundity of the vision and the boldness of the attempt to condense into a few lines of verse the paradox at the heart of Christianity. It is the paradox which has accompanied us on every step of our exploration: the relation between God's love and God's justice. Divine love, divine wisdom and divine justice are the creators of this place of damnation. In the history of Christian thought perhaps only John Calvin, two and a half centuries later, dared to place divine love and divine justice in so close a juxtaposition and explain one in terms of the other. But Dante's theology is radically different from that of the Reformer, whose doctrine of predestination he would utterly have repudiated. Here Dante is breathing narrative life into the classical, Catholic doctrine of human freedom, which had already been expounded by Thomas Aquinas. If one were to adopt the predestinarian theology of radical Calvinism, Dante's *Inferno* would be intolerable, its horrors unbearable. But the theological foundation upon which this place of torment is built is the doctrine of free will, the capacity in every human being of sound mind, however sinful, to choose freely and to be responsible for his or her own destiny. God does not operate in his world in a capricious way and does not commit souls to hell in an arbitrary fashion. Nor does he force any to choose either good or its absence. Damnation is the destiny of those who have chosen freely not to acknowledge the truth and love it when they see it. Dorothy L. Sayers wrote:

> We must also be prepared, while we are reading Dante, to accept the Christian and Catholic view of ourselves as responsible rational beings. We must abandon any idea that we are the slaves of chance, or environment, or our subconscious; any vague notion that good and evil are merely relative terms, or that conduct and opinion do not really matter; any comfortable persuasion that, however shiftlessly we muddle through life, it will somehow or other all come right on the night. We must try to believe that man's will is free, that he can consciously exercise choice, and that his choice can be decisive to all eternity.[9]

As we consider the way in which Dante imagined evil, we focus on the word *perduta* or 'lost' in the third line of the inscription. This word 'lost' appears again in the eighteenth line of the canto: 'We have come to the place where I have told you you will see the wretched people who have lost the good of intellect.' Thomas Aquinas spoke of evil as 'privation of form'. Dante here translates that as 'loss of intellect'; and 'intellect' has a special meaning here. The souls who find themselves in hell are not those who could not think; they are the creatures who have arrived at a state of being in which they are incapable, through the deliberate choices they have made throughout their lives, of distinguishing between what is true and what is false, between what is real and what is illusion. They can no longer tell the difference between good and bad; they imagine absence to be presence. This is the final stage of disorder. For Dante, the intellect, a concept of much greater richness than mere brain power, was the seat of the image of God in human nature: its loss would inevitably mean the loss of the image and so the loss of God. His *Inferno* is the attempt to imagine the doctrine of evil that is expounded by Thomas Aquinas: the absence of good; the perversion of order. Instead of abstract concepts of negation, there are the vivid, sensuous images of a world that is totally devoid of peace and harmony. The souls are finally and eternally prevented from attaining their true end. But what prevents them? Not God, for he has given each one of them the gift of freedom; nor the devil, for no one is in his power who has not deliberately willed himself or herself to be there.

Here we reach one of Dante's most arresting poetic achievements: his imagining of Satan. Like Thomas and Augustine, he accepted without question the veracity of the story of the fall of the angels, and evil could not have been persuasively imagined if supernatural malevolence had been omitted from the picture. But he was committed, by intellectual conviction, to a doctrine of evil as the privation of good, not to a dualistic world-picture in which man was a pawn in the conflict between the angels of light and the powers of the demons. The figure of Satan is to be found at the bottom of the pit that was Dante's Inferno. The two companions travel down through the circles of increasing loathsomeness towards that supremely evil creature. On the way the poet employs a vast array of images, many of them gathered from the legends and pictures popular in the culture of his day, absorbing them and using them to convey his own intensely personal understanding of orthodox theology. Edmund Wilson once remarked, in a quite different context, that an attentive reader should be able to extract an entire social history from a single lyric. So it is with *The Divine Comedy*: the social history of late medieval Europe is embedded in every canto – its superstitions and customs, its rituals and beliefs, its manners and politics, its fear of the demonic. But there is much more than a social history here: there is the transforming alchemy of the poetic imagination, a power which makes theology come alive. The demonic imagery of thirteenth-century carvings and paintings and the popular stories of devils and damnation are all harnessed to a single purpose, to the conveying of a theology of evil that is a long way removed from the dualism which they suggested in their original context. The speculations of the theologian are realised in the imagination of the poet. No one took evil more seriously than Dante, yet no one more scornfully dismissed theories that stated or implied that supernatural good and evil were locked in an eternal conflict, the outcome of which was still uncertain.

The bottom of the pit is not a roaring furnace of boiling heat but a region of ice, desolate and silent except for the sound of the wind that blows incessantly across the frozen lake; a place so cold that beards are stiff with frost and tears turn to ice as they fall from desolate eyes. Imprisoned in the centre of the lake of ice is the giant figure of Satan, beating his huge wings impotently while his three heads gnaw on the traitors Cassius, Brutus and Judas; a creature fallen from grace and beauty into hideous immobility; unable to do anything but contemplate his own fall; the embodiment, if such a thing were possible, of non-being. It is not, of course, possible, but it has been imagined. This is Satan's kingdom: the final numbing of all the senses; all feeling, all intellect is frozen; being itself is petrified; ultimate evil is seen as the ultimate stage of *privatio boni*.

He chose to ape the glory of the Trinity, and he has his choice: the monstrous three-headed parody lies fixed there in his inimitable self-will . . . the six wings of his immortal seraphhood beat savagely, powerless to lift him out of the ice of his own obduracy . . . That is the thing at the bottom: the idiot and slobbering horror . . . That is the picture seen by the poet who took evil seriously. And we cannot evade Dante by saying that we do not believe in that particular kind of judgement after death. For he himself said that his poem was indeed, *literally*, an account of what happens in the world beyond the grave, but, *allegorically*, an account of what happens within the soul. His Hell is the picture of an eternal possibility within the heart of man; and he adds that the gate to that Hell always stands wide open.[10]

# THE RETURN OF SATAN:
## 'EVIL BE THOU MY GOOD'

WILLIAM BLAKE'S comment on reading *Paradise Lost* was that John Milton, being 'a true poet', was 'of the Devil's party without knowing it'.[1] Opinion has been divided ever since. Although *Paradise Lost* was not published until the 1660s, as early as 1642 Milton (1608–74) had been contemplating a poetical work, perhaps even a drama, based on the story of Adam and Eve. In his own century there had been precedents for taking the story of the temptation of 'our first parents' in the Garden of Eden and giving it dramatic form. In 1601 the brilliant humanist lawyer, Grotius, had produced a Latin play on the subject, the third act of which contains a dialogue in which Satan tries to cajole Adam into friendship to form an alliance against God. In the face of Adam's resistance to his wheedling Satan threatens to destroy him. Milton was an admirer of Grotius and almost certainly knew the play, even if he had never seen it performed. Furthermore, the presentation of Satan in dramatic guise was becoming increasingly popular. As early as 1575 Tasso had represented a King of Darkness in his play, *Jerusalem Delivered*, and in English theatre there was already the example of Marlowe's *Dr. Faustus*, first seen in 1601. The Dutch poet Vondel had made Lucifer the central character of his own poetic drama in 1654, and the most famous Spanish playwright, Calderón, had put him into a play of 1637, *El magico prodigioso.* The seed had been planted in Milton's mind in the early 1640s, but nothing was to grow until two decades later.

In the meantime Milton, the pamphleteer and political theorist, busied himself with questions which were more pressing, such as the philosophical questions of freedom and constraint and the practical questions of the proper ordering of the new society which had come into being as the result of the Civil War and the establishment of Parliamentary rule. Turning with ever-increasing revulsion against his early Calvinism, he came more and more to uphold the notion that doctrinal orthodoxy 'is itself an anathema to Christian liberty . . . and an alien concept to the free Christian man'.[2] Paradoxically, this most sociable of characters, with a deep concern for the proper ordering of social life and a conviction about the necessity of orderly, responsible Parliamentary government, emerges more and more clearly as the century progresses as the champion of unrestrained individualism. Even in his unpublished treatise on Christian belief, *De Doctrina Christiana*, he gives the impression, in the very act of expounding right belief, that adherence to dogma is inimical to Christian freedom. This paradox finds its way into the heart of his greatest achievement, *Paradise Lost*, and is embodied in one of his most extraordinary creations, the figure of Satan. It was this paradox that Blake perceptively exposed a century later when he claimed that Milton 'wrote in fetters when he wrote of Angels of God, and at liberty when of Devils and Hell', a reading of *Paradise Lost* which was eagerly endorsed by some later commentators and just as eagerly denied by others.

The epic begins with a statement of its theological purpose – and it sounds orthodox enough:

> Of Mans first Disobedience and the Fruit
> Of that Forbidd'n Tree, whose mortal tast

Brought Death into the World, and all our woe,
With loss of *Eden*, till one greater Man
Restore us, and regain the blissful Seat,
Sing Heav'nly Muse . . .
. . . What in mee is dark
Illumin, what is low raise and support:
That to the highth of this great Argument
I may assert the Eternal Providence,
And justifie the wayes of God to men.[3]

It purports to be about the Fall of Adam and the loss
of innocence, but the story of the temptation is delayed for
thousands of lines of verse while the prologue to this
event is recounted. Books I, II and III contain the fall of
Satan and his angels, and the whole of Book II is set in Hell,
where the ruined legions of the rebellious host now
acrimoniously discuss their plight. It is difficult to determine
exactly who or what is at the centre of this poem. At this stage
'the very existence of man is only mooted as unhappy rumour'.[4]
Is it Adam and the disobedience of the human creature, as the
opening lines would have us believe, or is it in fact Satan
and his relationship with God? There can be no doubt that
it was a large part of Milton's purpose and triumph in *Paradise
Lost* to recreate in poetry a kind of physical reality of
the angelic kingdom. Like many before him, he contem-
plated the blessed obedience of the heavenly orders with delight,
but unlike those others, his fiercely individualistic cast of mind
led him into a portrayal of the attempted overthrow of that
order that was to pre-echo the figure of the isolated romantic
hero at odds with all dogma, convention, hierarchy, authority
and stability. Satan, early on, acquires features of intense
pathos and grandeur, of misery and, if we see what Blake saw,
dignity:

> . . . Farewell happy Fields
> Where Joy for ever dwells: Hail horrours, hail
> Infernal World, and thou profoundest Hell
> Receive they new Possessor: One who brings
> A mind not changed by Place or Time
> The mind is its own place, and in it self
> Can make a Heav'n of Hell, a Hell of Heav'n.[5]

But at the same time Milton cannot escape the notion of order as an irreducible good, something identified with the realm of the divine, and disorder as bad, something identified with the realm of evil. For while Milton paints the sympathetic portrait of the defiant archangel, at the same time he presents us with a figure who, out of sheer malice, does nothing more than bring misery and distress on all around him. Hating the innocent happiness of Adam and Eve and the harmony of Eden, he wills to destroy them and it. It is a peculiar situation: our sympathetic response to the fallen archangel is subverted by the actions of this heroic rebel; and it is in the context of this paradoxical situation that Milton produces his own understanding of the nature of evil.

The reason for Satan's rebellion had been the subject of much speculation in the writings of theologians from the very beginning of the Christian tradition. The Bible supplies us with very little in the way of information, and what little it tells us is ambiguous. Theologians felt free to speculate, and the early Fathers seem to be fairly evenly divided as to the cause. Origen located it in the sin of pride: the devil's desire to be 'as God'. Justin and Irenaeus, on the other hand, suggested that the cause was envy – that is, envy of the human beings God had created and of the love that he had bestowed on them. Scholastic theology in general followed the line of Origen and argued that the root of Satan's sin was pride. By the sixteenth century, however, another theory was current and was to be found in the teachings of one of the greatest and most influential of Catholic theologians, Francisco de Suarez. This was the theory that it was not out of envy of humanity that Satan rebelled, but out of envy of the Son of God. His desire was not to overthrow the omnipotent God and reign in his stead, but to be the equal of the beloved Son. Milton knew of this theory and, on the evidence of *Paradise Lost*, seems to have adopted it. This is the explanation of why, in the epic, it is the Son who, on behalf of the Father, takes up arms against the armies of Satan in the heavenly battle. It must be remembered, however, that in Book IV, as Satan muses upon his fate, he informs us that it was pride that caused his rebellion and defeat: 'Till Pride and worse Ambition threw me down / Warring in Heav'n against Heav'ns matchless King'.[6] There is a question here to which we shall return later, for it bears upon the problem of evil and Milton's approach to understanding it: whether we can take Satan at his word or whether he lacks the self-knowledge to perceive the truth about his own motives. Maurice Bowra, in his brilliant essay 'Milton and the Destiny of Man', curiously confuses envy and pride, as if he was unaware of the theological debates that had taken place down the centuries.

> Tradition told that pride was the cause of Satan's fall; Milton accepted this and made full use of it. He knew well what pride was, what illusions it can breed and what havoc it can create. So he sets the beginning of his whole story in Heaven, when Satan, incensed with envy and injured vanity at the elevation of the Son to share the Father's glory, prefers revolt to submission.[7]

Having failed in his attempt to overthrow the armies of the Son of God, Satan is cast out of Heaven and falls to 'bottomless perdition'. The divine ordering of the heavenly hierarchies remains in place; only in Pandemonium disorder reigns. Satan, impelled by his 'injured vanity', emerges from his quarrelsome kingdom to find something he can corrupt and subdue: man and woman in the Garden of Eden. Like a frustrated human being, full of hatred and anger, he turns destructively on a creature who is weaker, frailer – and blameless. The psychology is accurate and detestable; but Milton, unlike Dante, who depicted Satan as ultimately contemptible and repulsive in his futile degradation, still appears to encourage our sympathy and admiration for him in his heroic defiance of the Almighty. And he does this by providing him with a speech of overwhelming majesty and complexity as he flies across the universe on his way to accomplish his hateful ends. It begins with an evocation of the splendour of the sun and the beauty of the heavenly orders: the effect is to emphasise the dark solitariness of his own disordered life. It continues with a theological meditation on free will and the capacity inherent in all spiritual beings to choose to reject the known good for something of lesser value: in this case and at this moment in the story, self-esteem. The 'stance' of the author in this crucial soliloquy is all important: Milton is trying to provide his readers with a character who is psychologically convincing (we still do not know how far Satan's perceptions are to be trusted) while demonstrating the theological proposition that evil can be deliberately chosen – even in the conscious knowledge that it is evil. The extraordinary speech is a poetic rendering of what Charles Williams called 'the deliberate acquiescence in a divided consciousness': to know and refuse to know at the same time.

> Hads't thou the same free Will and Power to stand?
> Thou hadst: whom hast thou then or what to accuse,
> But Heav'n's free Love dealt equally to all?
> Be then his Love accurst, since love or hate,
> To mee alike, it deals eternal woe,
> Nay curst be thou; since against his thy will
> Chose freely what it now so justly rues.
> Mee miserable! which way shall I flie

> Infinite wrath and infinite despair?
> Which way I flie is Hell; myself am Hell;
> And in the lowest deep a lower deep
> Still threatening to devour me op'ns wide,
> To which the Hell I suffer seems a Heav'n.[8]

The soliloquy ends with those words which are at the centre of the paradox of Satan's character and Milton's treatment of evil. Again the 'stance' of the author is of crucial importance. Is Milton speaking through Satan, using the character he has created to voice his own theological viewpoint, or must the character be read as 'character', dramatically articulating an intellectual position from which the author is deliberately distanced?

> So farwel Hope, and with Hope farwel Fear,
> Farwel Remorse: all Good to me is lost;
> Evil be thou my Good; by thee at least
> Divided Empire with Heav'ns King I hold,
> By thee, and more then half perhaps will reign;
> As Man ere long, and this new World shall know.[9]

C. S. Lewis' comment on this in his *Preface to Paradise Lost* is as follows: 'What we must see in Milton's Satan is the horrible co-existence of a subtle and incessant intellectual activity combined with an incapacity to understand anything.'[10] Neither Lewis nor Charles Williams, whose interpretation Lewis is elaborating here, denies the pathos or the grandeur of the speech, or that Satan is the most fully achieved of the characters of the poem. But each draws attention to the possibility that Satan is trying to build his existence on a lie: that the reasons he gives for his actions and motives and the means by which he explains his nature are dishonest and self-delusory. This is self-justification of the worst kind. The lie is that which he tells himself (and others) – that he could exist without God and that evil can be a means of sustaining existence. This lie is enlarged in his claim that he will be able to hold 'Divided Empire with Heav'ns King'. On the surface this looks like a distinct possibility: he is, after all, flying towards Eden, where he will persuade Adam and Eve to disobey God. Does this place the human pair under his control? Will the world of human affairs come under his rule? Evil, thus embodied in Satan, could become a real power in opposition to that of God. As we have seen, a substantial part of the Christian tradition accepted this interpretation and adopted a modified dualism: man was caught in the supernatural struggle between the power of God and that of Satan; life on earth was part of a celestial conflict. Did Milton too accept this interpretation? Both Williams and Lewis deny this. Both argue that Satan's apparent embracing of evil as a principle of existence is actually absurd and that Milton knew it. The resounding line, 'Evil be thou my Good', is deliberately intended to be a statement of self-contradiction. This reading of the poem is argued on the grounds that Milton accepted the theological position that evil was *privatio boni* and had no real existence. Only the good has being, and since there is only the good to know, evil cannot be known, still less can it consciously and intelligently be made a principle of existence. Satan's desire to be what he is not and still remain in being is an impossibility. Any attempt to embrace such a self-contradictory principle will result in self-annihilation.

The problem for the reader is whether Milton did in fact interpret evil in this way – that is, as privation – and, therefore, consciously created the character of Satan as the poetic embodiment of this theory. At first sight we might doubt it. Milton had addressed the subject of the Fall of Man and the problem of evil before, most notably in 1644 in the *Areopagitica*. He wrote:

It was from the rinde of one apple tasted, that the knowledge of good and evill as two twins cleaving together leapt forth into the World. And perhaps this is that doom which *Adam* fell into of knowing good and evill, that is to say of knowing good by evill. As therefore the state of man now is: what wisdom can there be to choose, what continence to forbeare without the knowledge of good and evil.[11]

In this argument it would seem that evil becomes a necessity if Adam (we) are to have freedom of choice (there is no mention of Satan in the *Areopagitica*; supernatural temptation has been banished from Eden in this account of the Genesis story), for without the possibility of choosing between either good or evil, mankind cannot be said to possess freedom in any real sense. But what exactly is meant by evil in this context? At one point in this essay Milton declares his preference for the poet Edmund Spenser as a moral, and perhaps theological teacher over the medieval theologians, Duns Scotus and Thomas Aquinas. It was well known that Thomas had taught and developed a doctrine of evil as the absence of good; was Milton consciously rejecting Thomas' theory here? William Blake, that thoroughgoing dualist, thought so; moreover, Satan is so vital a figure in *Paradise Lost* that it is hard not to read the existence of a certain kind of dualism in Milton's picture. The war in heaven, however peculiar and ludicrous it may seem to us, may have been taken seriously by its author; at the same time it must be admitted that it would have been extremely difficult to make privation, the absence of good, dramatically interesting. We must be careful. Milton was also profoundly influenced by Augustine, who had unambiguously declared, in many places, that evil was the absence of good. We must also remember that it was Lucifer, the creation of the Almighty, who fell, not some self-existent principle of evil who rose spontaneously in opposition to the goodness of God.

The transformation of Satan in the course of the poem is also significant. He starts out as the figure of the hero: imposing, dominating, tragic in his fall. That is not how he ends. We witness his steady degradation as he assumes various shapes. Entering the earth's atmosphere, he becomes a toad and then a snake. Even when he returns to Hell to boast of the triumphant achievement of his mission, he can gain no satisfaction from the announcement, for before he can receive and acknowledge the plaudits of his audience, his companions have, themselves, been transmogrified into serpents. With mordant and macabre humour Milton fills the spaces of the infernal kingdom with a wordless hiss. The choice of evil as a principle of existence has resulted in this: humiliation. This is no victory for Satan; the grasp at glory has turned out to be impossible to achieve. One cannot read this, despite the apparent tragic stature of the earlier descriptions, as other than Milton's rejection of Satan, and, indeed, the rejection of all notions of heroism that are constructed upon concepts of power and self-determination – a position he will explicate in detail in the later works, *Paradise Regained* and *Samson Agonistes*. Did Milton, perhaps, change his mind about Satan half way through the writing of *Paradise Lost*? I think not, but if we take this progressive degradation seriously it means that we have to read those earlier passages, especially those in which Satan soliloquises about his own condition, with far greater sceptical attention. There is, I would suggest, an assumption of the tragic mask by Satan to hide the essential emptiness of his being: the speeches are full of pretence and self-delusion.

I think it is quite proper to argue, as Charles Williams does, that Satan's fall was brought about not only by envy or pride but also by a failure of intelligence. Here Maurice Bowra agrees with him: Satan's pride darkens his reason. 'Persuasive as his words are, they are based on false assumptions and show that he lives with darkness and lies'; and 'Satan has no real or reasonable principle even in his malice.'[12] I would further argue that for Milton the lies and delusions are not consequent upon the pride or envy, but may even be seen, in some sense, as the cause of the pride or envy. Satan's failure lies not only in refusing to accept his status in the heavenly order but in not being intelligent enough to see what his status is.

That Milton should see that the fall of Satan could be caused by a failure of intelligence should not come as a surprise, given the shape of his intellectual development. His revulsion against the Calvinism of his day and his close contacts with the humanist learning on the Continent of Europe drew him further and further away from the traditional (i.e. orthodox) readings of Christian doctrine, especially those of the Trinity and the Atonement. I have already mentioned the *Areopagitica*: it is clear from that text that Milton was already placing high value on the human capacity to reason and arrive at the truth by the processes of the intelligence. It was the intellect, correctly used, that enabled one to discern the difference between right and wrong, good and evil. One would not be incorrect to call this a kind of Gnosticism, but it is not, of course, a Gnosticism that envisages the achievement of salvation by the means of the possession of esoteric knowledge, or initiation into a secret society whose members, superior to the rest of humanity, believed that only they had a hold on the truth. Milton's Gnosticism was that of the educated humanist, which consisted in believing that reason was the distinguishing mark of the human being and, rightly used, would direct the human soul infallibly to the truth. That truth, available to all, would ensure salvation.

Of course, I have over-simplified his position, but, in essence, this became his mature thinking. So in the later work, *Paradise Regained*, Christ is represented as the mirror image of both Adam and Satan. Both had made wrong choices out of a false apprehension of reality. It is the Son of God who perceives the true nature of things as they are and so is able to overcome the temptations offered by Satan in the wilderness. Whereas in *Paradise Lost* Adam's intelligence is corrupted by submitting to Eve, who, in turn, has been seduced by Satan into believing his lies, in *Paradise Regained* Christ's intelligence remains unshakeable in its hold upon what really is, and this opens the way to the ultimate defeat of Satan and the dispersion of all illusions brought about by the spread of evil. Salvation is wrought not by sacrifice but by transformation in the truth; not by a life surrendered, but by knowledge gained. It may not be orthodox Christianity, but it is what Milton believed.

It is, fundamentally, a doctrine of salvation by illumination: the capacity of the free mind to perceive clearly what things are true and what are false. There is thus a sense in which Adam and Eve are innocent of the necessity of making choices in their original condition; Satan, in Milton's redaction of the Eden story, is necessary to them if they are to grow up into that condition in which every moment of life entails a choice. We are back to the thought of the *Areopagitica*, in which it is claimed that we cannot know the good unless we are aware of its opposite. Adam and Eve, making their way out of Eden, are by no means crushed and ruined creatures (unlike the rebel angels); they are embarking on a journey which will entail the discovery of the necessity of separating out good and evil, and they will arrive at a state of enlightenment.

All this having been said, there remains, however, an uncomfortable awareness of an ambivalence embodied in *Paradise Lost* which is never really resolved. In the end I cannot accept in its entirety the interpretation of Williams and Lewis. On the one hand, Milton stands with the great Anglican thinker Richard Hooker in his concept of order. He knew Hooker's *Laws of Ecclesiastical Polity* well and much of his own work can be read as a reaction to this vastly influential treatise. On the other hand, he had stepped away from the medieval world-view of which Hooker could be said to be the last major exponent, and from the church which Hooker had helped to bring into being. We may even see Milton at the start of the process of the desacralisation of the universe by investing the most famous of the angelic beings, Satan, with such startlingly human properties. He could not imagine Heaven. Most commentators have drawn attention to the awkwardness of the poetry that portrays God, his Son and the heavenly beings. Comparing him with Dante, for example, it is almost as though both Heaven and Hell were beyond the reach of his imagination. He could do many things that Dante could not do, but he could not achieve, poetically, either Heaven or Hell except in terms that display his own philosophical ambivalence. His is actually a divided consciousness – which is what makes him so fascinating a case study. He both wants to retain the concept of order, so vital to the tradition he had inherited from Dante and Hooker, and, at the same time, to assert the necessity of abandoning it in favour of an individualistic psychology by which the acquisition of knowledge, independent of all received schemes, is the means to personal salvation. In the end I do not think he believed in the reality of evil except as a state of mind.

This divided consciousness surfaces from time to time in the three central characters of his epic – which brings us to that line which is of such crucial importance for our reading of the poem:

> The mind is its own place, and in itself
> Can make a Heav'n of Hell, a Hell of Heav'n.[13]

Is Satan deceiving himself in this statement? Or is this Milton presenting a new perception of our knowledge of reality? Do Heaven and Hell really exist, objectively, or are they states of the mind only? Is this a decisive movement away from orthodox Christian definitions of the being of God and creaturely relations with him, or is this another example of Satan's failure to 'understand anything'? It is very difficult to be sure, but we should remember that Milton cared nothing for orthodoxy and that his close contemporary was the philosopher, John Locke. It is true that Locke's *Essay concerning Human Understanding* was not published until 1690, sixteen years after Milton's death, but discussion about the nature of perception and the structures of the human mind was already in the air and had been an important subject in philosophical conversation since the appearance of Descartes' *Discourse on Method* in 1637. One cannot avoid the impression of ambivalence in Milton. At the level of the images and the narrative of *Paradise Lost* he accepts the medieval order of the universe; at the level of philosophical conviction he is already beginning a process of interiorisation, of locating reality within the perceiving and experiencing self. Evil, on this analysis, may well be embodied in the figure of Satan, but it has ceased to exist as a supernatural possibility; it has to be located within the individual human mind. The whole epic becomes a vast metaphor of the interior struggle of the heroic individual with himself or herself. On this reading *Paradise Lost* becomes a significant text in its representation of that movement towards interiority which was to gain momentum throughout the eighteenth and nineteenth centuries.

This very ambivalence prepared the way for those romantic interpretations of society and religion exemplified by William Blake: the belief that heroic humanism was always in rebellion, that hierarchy was always oppressive, that individualism was the characteristic of true humanity, that obedience and humility were worthy only of the stupid; and the childish notion, beloved of second-rate imaginations, that evil is always more interesting than goodness. Now, I do not think, for a minute, that Milton intended these consequences or would have rejoiced to see them, but one can see how his portrayal of the figure of Satan in *Paradise Lost* could lead in all these directions.

# 7

## EVERYTHING
## FOR THE BEST

An EPIDEMIC in Algeria in the 1940s may well have given Albert Camus the idea of writing *The Plague*, a novel in which the problem of evil in one of its most acute forms, innocent suffering, could be portrayed and discussed. An earthquake in Portugal two centuries earlier had given Francois-Marie Arouet, known as Voltaire, the opportunity of writing a novelistic satire in which exactly the same issues could be addressed.

In 1755 there occurred an event, unexpected and devastating, which shocked the whole of the civilised world and which, in retrospect, can be seen to have been a major cause of the change which came over European sensibility in the later part of the eighteenth century. On All Saints' Day 1755, as the people of the city of Lisbon were at mass, there was an earthquake in which, it was estimated, more than 50,000 people were killed and more than half of the city was destroyed.

The terrible loss of life and the wreckage of the city immediately threw into high relief, in an already sceptical age, the question of how a good and loving God could permit such an occurrence. A cruel twist was given to the dilemma for believers – one which was gleefully seized upon by the opponents of religion – in the fact that the disaster had occurred at the very time when the devout were at prayer and had lit candles which, as the buildings shook and toppled, started the fires that swept rapidly through the streets of timber-framed houses, causing as much damage as the quake itself.

Into the storm of philosophical and theological controversy that followed in the wake of this disaster stepped Voltaire (1694–1778), already celebrated throughout Europe as a man of letters, with a work entitled *Poeme sur le desastre de Lisbonne* (published in 1756). In the preface to the poem he examined the arguments of those attempting an explanation of the catastrophe and, in particular, scrutinised contemptuously the efforts of the fashionable philosophers of the day known as the 'Optimists'. These thinkers were trying to make sense of the suffering with their doctrine of 'everything for the best' in this 'best of all possible worlds', even earthquakes which killed tens of thousands of people. Two years later he returned to the attack in a different and more deadly mode with a fictional lampoon of the philosophy he despised: *Candide* (1759). This book is not merely an attack on traditional religion; in the character of Dr Pangloss, Voltaire ridiculed both the notion of belief in a God as a just and loving Creator of the universe and, more particularly, as in his poem of 1756, the extrapolation of traditional theism in the form of the cosmology and moral philosophy of the Optimists.

We are told that Dr Pangloss 'taught metaphysico-theologo-cosmolo-nigology' and that 'He proved incontestably that there is no effect without cause, and that in this best of all possible worlds, his lordship's country seat was the most beautiful of mansions . . .'[1] But the gentle hero, Candide, is ejected from this earthly paradise, and after several unpleasant adventures is reunited with Pangloss, in whose company he travels to Lisbon at the time of the earthquake. In the midst of the terror of falling roofs and crumbling foundations, Pangloss is found asking the question, 'What can be "the sufficient reason" for this phenomenon?'[2] Candide can only answer, 'The Day of Judgement has come.' It clearly hasn't, of course, and as the companions sit among the ruins of the city, weeping over the devastation that surrounds them, Pangloss offers

> the assurance that things could not be otherwise. 'For all this,' said he, 'is a manifestation of the rightness of things, since if there is a volcano at Lisbon it could not be anywhere else. For it is impossible for things not to be where they are, because everything is for the best.' A little man in black, an officer of the Inquisition, who was sitting behind Pangloss, turned to him and politely said: 'It appears, Sir, that you do not believe in original sin; for if all is for the best, there can be no such thing as the fall of Man and eternal punishment.'
>
> 'I humbly beg your Excellency's pardon,' replied Pangloss, still more politely, 'but I must point out that the fall of Man and eternal punishment enter, of Necessity, into the scheme of the best of all possible worlds.'[3]

In *Candide*, as in much of what Voltaire wrote, the tone of the prose carries the force of the message, and this mockery deliberately masks the fact that Voltaire found the 'explanation' of the earthquake and its terrible consequences offered by Pangloss as unsatisfactory as was the explanation of the plague and the dying children given to Dr Rieux by the priest Paneloux in Camus' *The Plague*. But the lightness of touch in *Candide* does nothing to hide Voltaire's knowledge of the philosophical issues in the controversies he was satirising, nor his contempt for their conclusions. Behind this little debate between Pangloss and the officer of the Inquisition lies a much larger debate which had begun in the previous century.

At the centre of this debate were the theories of one of the most brilliant mathematicians of the age: Gottfried Leibniz (1646–1716). In 1720 he had published his *Essais de théodicée sur la bonte de Dieu, la liberté de l'homme et l'origine de mal* (Essays on Theodicy, about the benevolence of God, the freedom of man, and the origin of evil). It is probable that Leibniz himself had coined the word 'theodicy' to 'justify the ways of God to man'. In this immensely complicated work of philosophical theology he tried to answer increasingly strongly held and cleverly articulated theories which maintained that the concept of a loving God and an omnipotent Creator were incompatible with the existence of evil. It is the age-old question in a seventeenth-century setting, and Leibniz proceeded to answer it in a seventeenth-century manner. His answer looks decidedly odd in many ways to us today, and to appreciate it and understand the reasons for his making it in the way he did, we shall have to set Leibniz against his background. We shall then, also, be in a better position to evaluate Voltaire's satiric rejection of much that Leibniz stood for.

John Milton died in 1674. Thirteen years later, in a mellifluous hymn of praise to the art of music, his younger contemporary, John Dryden, who had been received into the Roman Catholic Church in 1686, sounded the key-note of the era that was later to be called the Age of Enlightenment:

> From harmony, from heavenly harmony
> This universal frame began:
> From harmony to harmony
> Through all the compass of the notes it ran,
> The diapason closing full in MAN.
>
> (*Song for St Cecilia's Day*)

The poem was not only a celebration of the art of music but an enthusiastic acclamation of the Newtonian cosmology: that concept of the universe which was to dominate physics and astronomy for more than 200 years and which helped to shape, perhaps even determine, the thinking and self-understanding of a whole culture for much longer. It would become impossible for any serious philosopher or scientist to ignore Newtonian explanations for the structure of the universe from the beginning of the seventeenth century onwards. (Alexander Pope amusingly, but accurately, gauged the effect of Newton's work on succeeding generations in his epitaph for the great mathematician: 'Nature, and Nature's laws lay hid in night: / God said, *Let Newton be!* and all was light.') In the same year that Dryden's *Song for St Cecilia* appeared Newton had published his first edition of the work that contained his ideas on the laws of planetary motions and universal gravity: *Philosophiae Naturalis Principia Mathematica*. Newton did not invent the notion of the universe as a complex machine-like structure, but he perfected it and, in this work seemed to demonstrate its unassailable veracity. As one writer comments, 'The mechanical idea of nature had been fully worked out before his time; he accepted it without question and made it the basis of his work. The principal thing he added to it was mathematical precision.'[4]

It was not so much Newton's mathematical account of the universe that Dryden was celebrating as the principle of the rational, mechanical ordering of the universe: an order that could be known, and the movements of the planets predicted, by the mind of man. Both the sense of the arbitrariness of cosmological arrangements and the sense of the unexpected irruptions into the cosmos of the extraordinary or the miraculous were banished in this new vision of the world. Human beings could now be seen to inhabit a universe which was 'reasonable', which operated by identifiable physical and mathematical laws; a universe in which uncertainty, fear and mystery would be endured only by those not prepared to accept the facts of the new science.

Today we live in an age when the Newtonian world-view has been challenged, and in some senses, superseded by modern physics, and the mechanistic model of the universe has been discarded as a questionable, if not misleading concept inimical to true religion. So it is interesting to us to find the great humane, religious spirits of the Augustan age – Addison, Pope and Dryden – hailing Newton's world-view as a marvellous truth which revealed the world as it really was. Dryden had already become a Roman Catholic by the time he wrote his ode, but he saw no reason to suppose that the new discoveries would threaten the truths of the old religion. From our vantage-point we may be puzzled by this and see contradictions but, clearly, he saw none. Similarly, Joseph Addison (1672–1719) wrote luminously of the beauty of this vision of the universe in an ode that became one of the best-loved hymns in English churches:

> The spacious firmament on high,
> With all the blue ethereal sky,
> And spangled heavens, a shining frame,
> Their great Original proclaim.

The intricate mechanism of a universe obedient to natural law, rational and observable, seemed to him a thing of wonder and the clearest evidence of rational Mind behind the cosmos, ordering all things for good and ensuring the peace and harmony of human life. The very regularity of the laws of Nature seemed only to confirm humanity in its belief in the comprehensibility of the Divine Being. The veils of mystery that had surrounded the God of previous, more superstitious ages were brushed thankfully aside in this new apprehension of the relationship between the world and its Maker. One needed only to look at the wonderful rationality of the cosmos to understand the true nature of the Mind that had been responsible for it.

Newton himself was profoundly, if perplexingly, religious, and his famous work of 1687 contained evidence of theological convictions. For him the very laws which inexorably governed the solar system just as inexorably indicated the existence of a divine intelligence. But he found that several aspects of ortho-dox Christianity could not be accommodated in his new perspectives on the universe and its workings. His curious and susceptible imagination, on the one hand, led him into bizarre millenarian speculations and a preoccupation with alchemy, while at the same time his extreme rationalism brought him close to identifying the eternal and infinite life of God with the eternity and infinity of the world. But it was the doctrine of providence which was to prove the most intractable of problems. In what sense could the God of Newton's universe be said to be operative and active in his own creation? How could he act personally in a world which was governed by inflexible laws? And how was the concept of evil to be fitted into this picture of the world? Was evil a concept that could have any reference to reality at all? In a well-known passage from the *Principia* Newton seems to approach the subject when he speaks about the 'dominion' of God, who 'governs all things, not as the soul of the world, but as Lord over all . . .' But the sentences are cloudy with rhetoric and the question of whether the relationship of the Lord of Creation to his creation can be described in moral terms – essential in any attempt to deal with the problem of evil – is left unanswered. In a curious way we are thrown back to the framework of the book of Job. Job poses all his questions to God in the language of morality: 'How can the Lord be just and righteous if the world is a place of undeserved suffering?' God answers in the languauge that sets aside morality: 'I am the Creator of the universe.' In just such a way might Newton's God have answered those who were maimed or made homeless in the Lisbon earthquake of 1755.

Leibniz saw this particular problem much more clearly than Newton, whose doctrine of creation he was known to have shared. While Newton left the question of evil hanging in the air, Leibniz placed it at the very centre of his philosophy. One sees him struggling to answer, in his own highly sophisticated, rationalistic way, the existential problem which Newton avoided. Evil is thus described by him in three ways: metaphysical, physical and moral. In essence metaphysical evil can be equated with finitude – that is, with the fact that all things decline inevitably into death. Physical evil encompasses all the suffering that is the consequence of 'natural' disaster: floods, famine, earthquakes, volcanoes. His explanation for this state of affairs is surprisingly orthodox and one which appears in a multitude of different guises in the Judeao-Christian tradition. Suffering is intended, in the first place, as a punishment for guilt (but Job asks, 'How am I guilty?') and secondly as a means of purification in order that a greater good may arise out of the suffering willingly accepted.

The third kind of evil – moral evil – is a development of the explanation already classically expounded by Thomas Aquinas but here translated into the vocabulary of Leibniz's own theology of creation. It rests upon the concept of freedom. The wilful acts of depravity by human beings occur because all persons are free to choose evil instead of the good – and many do. This, in fact, is the central plank of his argument. The world God made was a world in which freedom could exist: if this freedom is real and not illusory, then real evil must also be a possibility. He spoke quite simply here: that it was sufficient to show that a world which contained evil would be better than a world without evil, for a world without evil would be a world in which there was no freedom. It is by this route that we reach the doctrine of this world being the 'best of all possible worlds', not by some facile optimism which ignores the reality of suffering. God was, therefore, responsible for evil in the world, for he was its Creator, but he could not, logically, be morally culpable in the sense that he was the cause of evil deeds. If he had created a world in which there was no possibility of evil, it would be a world in which there was no freedom, and it would not, by definition, be the best of all possible worlds.

We may feel that Job's and Dr Rieux's question and complaints are still unanswered by this attempt to explain the existence of evil, for the link between human freedom and natural disaster is unconvincingly demonstrated, but the cultivated minds of the eighteenth century found this 'reading' of life extraordinarily persuasive. And just as a quite different account of reality – dualism – and a quite different perspective on the problem of evil had informed much of the religious devotion and the art of the Middle Ages, so this 'optimistic' philosophy quickly found its way into the prayers, the art, and the literature of the eighteenth century. It became part of the European imagination and we find it everywhere. In 1728 William Law, already famous for his writings on the spiritual life, published the book that was to find its way into thousands of English homes and have as much influence on the lives of English Christians as *Pilgrim's Progress*. It was *A Serious Call to a Holy and Devout Life*. In chapter 22 he enters briefly into the problem of evil, placing it firmly in the framework of the doctrine of Providence. The chapter heading instructs the reader to contemplate at this hour of the day (three o'clock) 'resignation to the Divine pleasure. The nature and duty of conformity to the will of God, in all our actions and designs.' Law considers the virtue of patience and the necessity of believing that the Lord desires our happiness and good. Temptations to complain against God when all is not going well must be resisted, as they are signs of ignorance, a failure to recognise the infinite goodness in the providence of God. 'Whenever, therefore, you find yourself disposed to uneasiness, or murmuring at anything that is the effect of God's providence over us, you must look upon yourself as denying either the wisdom or the goodness of God.' This injunction is not remarkable in the history of Christian piety, nor is Law's doctrine of providence original in the history of Christian theology, but a few lines further on there occur phrases that embody the special quality of the spirituality of the age: a kind of optimistic serenity peculiar to the eighteenth century which echoes, however unconsciously, the philosophy of Leibniz:

> Every man . . . is to believe, that it is the effect of God's great wisdom and goodness, that the world itself was formed at such a particular time, and in such a manner; that the general ordering of nature, the whole frame of things, is contrived and formed in the best manner. He is to believe that God's providence over states and kingdoms, times and seasons, is all for the best: that revolutions of state and changes of empire, the rise and fall of monarchies, persecutions, wars, famines, and plagues, are all permitted and conducted by God's providence to the general good of man in this state of trial.[5]

What had begun in 1687 with John Dryden's *Song for St Cecilia's Day* reached what might almost be called an apotheosis six years after the appearance of William Law's *A Serious Call* in Alexander Pope's *Essay on Man* of 1734. This has been described as 'the principal English philosophical poem of the eighteenth century'.[6]

The *Essay on Man* is a theodicy in verse: there is even a deliberate allusion to Milton's *Paradise Lost* in the opening section, Epistle 1, as the poet explains his purpose, which is 'to vindicate the ways of God to Man'.[7] Pope's 'vindication', however, is totally different from Milton's 'justification'. Their idea of evil is as different as their idea of what constitutes the good life. Pope's theodicy, in substantial ways, is even a contradiction of Milton's, and he shows no interest in returning to the primal myth of the Garden of Eden and the Fall. Evil, for Pope, needs no aetiological explanation even though, as a Christian believer, he acknowledges the presence of the myth in the tradition of his religion. The wickedness of individual men and women might indeed be the result of a sin of pride, but the apparent disorder of the universe is precisely that, 'apparent', and could not be caused either by some primeval act of disobedience in an earthly paradise or by the premundane rebellion of an arch-angel. All notions of dualism are swept aside in the surge of Pope's imagination. The most famous lines of the poem encap-sulate his approach to the problem:

> All nature is but art, unknown to thee,
> All chance, discretion which thou canst not see,
> All discord, harmony not understood,
> All partial evil, universal good.
> And spite of pride, in erring reason's spite,
> One truth is clear, whatever is, is right.[8]

These lines end the first Epistle. The phrase 'whatever is, is right'[9] appears again in the last section of the poem, the fourth Epistle. We do not know if Pope was directly acquainted with the writings of Leibniz, but we know of his admiration for Newton, and the controlling ideas of the *Essay on Man* could only have evolved in a culture that had been strongly influenced by the astronomy of Newton and the philosophy of Leibniz. 'Then say not Man's imperfect, Heav'n in fault; / Say rather, Man's as perfect as he ought.'[10]

However, Pope's attempt at giving a comprehensive vindi-cation of 'the ways of God to Man' contains two intentions that are not easily reconcilable. First, he aims to show that in the best of all possible worlds there will, inevitably, be dishar-mony and degrees of imperfection; that 'evil' is somehow inherent in creation. But, secondly, he wants to show that it is only on account of the incompleteness of our knowledge and the feebleness of our understanding that we see the world as imperfect and unharmonious. We sin the sin of Job when we question the Almighty about the miserable disorder of the world. We are conceited and presumptuous if we deceive our-selves into imagining that our faulty reason and frail intelligence can penetrate the mystery of the divine mind and perceive the harmony of the divine activity. Hence the rebuke, so often misinterpreted and misquoted, that comes at the opening of the second Epistle: 'Know then thyself, presume not God to scan; / The proper study of mankind is man.' The problem of the existence of evil has here been resolved into a problem of faulty knowledge and inaccurate perception. The universe we inhabit is a universe whose miseries and disasters are devastating only when considered from our own inadequate point of view; our sight is only partial sight; we should know differently and better if we could see the universal plan of God. (Voltaire, of course, and countless others, thought that our own point of view was precisely the place where we had to make sense of things.)

It is an argument frequently heard in the mouths of believers, but it has rarely been expressed with such breathtaking artfulness; and it is not without its strength. A. D. Nuttall comments:

> Today the same students who will eagerly 'accept the universe' or thrill to Blake's 'Everything that lives is holy' are instantaneously repelled by Pope's line. Yet Pope's formulation is simply the most radical, the most absolute, the most correct. The others, it might be said, survive because they are prudently involved in a Romantic haze.[11]

Our difficulty with the optimism of the *Essay on Man* arises partly, as Nuttall suggests, out of the manner of the presentation of the argument. It seems, sometimes, as though Pope is suggesting that all our agonies and anger would cease if we managed to see things from another perspective and give things their proper names, or if, in the style of Dr Pangloss, we could see the 'sufficient cause' of all our ills. Pope was not as optimistic as this and was well aware of the hatefulness of human misery, but however he may have modified his views and conveyed a darker picture of life in other places, those assertions of the *Essay on Man* remain vividly expressive of a vital and irrepressible strain in Christian culture at a particular moment of its history. Which brings us back to Voltaire's criticism of that strain in *Candide*.

Even when we know that Voltaire was not doing justice to the complexity and sophistication of Leibniz's philosophy in his lampoon, that he was aiming his darts at more naive and more obviously callous followers of the great mathematician, his satire bites deeply into the theodicy of Leibniz and the more orthodox Christian theories. It is true that in *Candide* the powerful 'argument from freedom' is virtually ignored. Nonetheless, implicit in the satire is the justifiable complaint that, in the schemes of Leibniz and Pope or anyone else embracing this argument, there is no logical connection between the free choice of human beings for good or evil and natural disasters like earthquakes and plagues. One can see, and accept, that human wickedness can be, and frequently is, the cause of indescribable suffering, but how can it be held responsible for painful death by cancer? or deformities of mind or body that have genetic origins? or the failure of crops through drought or flooding? Voltaire abandoned, early on in his life, belief in the Christian God of love and justice: in the end his hero, Candide, decides to renounce metaphysical speculation. In a last answer to Dr Pangloss he puts aside all theories and says, 'We must go and work in the garden.' But in the Judaeo-Christian tradition it was in a garden that evil first took root.

In this scheme, the best of all possible worlds, dualism disappears: Satan is banished from the universe of the Enlightenment, Romanticism was to bring him back in a strange guise.

# EVIL ROMANTICISED:
# THE LURE OF DEPRAVITY

THE GREAT POPULAR successes of the culture of any age often, in retrospect, prove to be the most ephemeral products of their own eras. Who, now, reads the novels of Mrs Radcliffe? Or listens to the music of Antonio Salieri? Who, now, can recall the names of any of those painters who were preferred to the Impressionists in the Paris Salon exhibitions of the 1870s? In 1827 John Keble published *The Christian Year*, a collection of devotional verses based on the Church of England's liturgical year, the calendar of the Book of Common Prayer. Its success was astonishing: by 1866, the year of Keble's death, the anthology had sold over a quarter of a million copies and passed through more than ninety editions. Today it is virtually unknown and seldom read. In nineteenth-century France the success of Ernest Renan's *La Vie de Jésus* was even more spectacular. Within a year of its first appearance in 1863 it had run through eleven editions; by the end of the century it is estimated that over half a million copies had been bought. Today it is remembered only by those who have an interest in the history of ideas or the history of nineteenth-century France. We may not, today, find either of these books enlightening, attractive or appealing, but the fact of their phenomenal success tells us a great deal about the culture of the age in which they achieved such acclaim.

Of the two it is undoubtedly Renan's *La Vie de Jésus* that is the more significant. At the risk of over-simplification, one could say that *The Christian Year* held up a mirror to what was already happening in English religion; it gently encouraged the reader along a path that was already being taken; it helped to define, but did not create a change in religious sensibility. *La Vie de Jésus*, on the other hand, did bring about something new. Owen Chadwick refers to its publication as a landmark. 'It was the most famous book in France during the nineteenth century, and until about 1900 its author was the most famous of French writers.'[1] In this 'biography' of Jesus Christ, Renan was intent on bringing the figure of Jesus 'down to earth', close to the lives of the ordinary readers of books in French society. Supernatural elements of the story disappeared, the Lord was stripped of the mysterious attributes of divinity: in the process the central character was turned, as the more hostile critics were quick to observe, into a man who bore more resemblance to the culti-vated gentlemen of nineteenth-century Paris than the itinerant preacher of first-century Palestine. The manner of the writing of this particular book and its reception by scholarly opinion is of comparatively little importance to us here: what is of importance are the theological and philosophical foundations upon which this account of the life of Jesus was laid.

Renan's was a complicated personality. His intellectual and emotional roots lay in that movement we call Romanticism, but he is quoted as saying, 'I was predestined to be what I am, a romantic in protest against romanticism.'[2] By the 1840s it was clear that his future was not with the seminarians of St Sulpice and the Catholic Church. He was already deeply indebted, intellectually, to the Romantic thinkers of previous decades, yet, at the same time, enamoured of the spirit of enquiry that characterised movements in the natural sciences. The super-naturalism of traditional religion could not easily be reconciled with the new spirit of the age or his own changing perceptions of reality. In 1849 he had begun a work that took nearly forty years to complete, *L'Avenir de la Science*, in which some of the complexity of his personality is demonstrated. He criticises the thinkers of the Enlightenment for their lack of imagination in a manner typical of Romantic poets and philosophers: they are indifferent to the sublime and the infinite. 'The mystery of origins, the prodigies of instinct, the spirit that moves crowds, the spontaneous in all its forms passed them by.'[3]

This sounds the authentic Romantic note: an impatience with eighteenth-century mechanistic philosophies, the longing for sensation, the emphasis on emotion, the yearning for that which cannot be fully explained by reason. At the same time there is a rejection of the forms of orthodox piety and the attempt to replace traditional religious dogma with a scientific theory of human nature. As the sublime and the infinite could not be found in either Christian worship or in the cosmologies of Enlightenment philosophy, it could only be discovered in a dynamic process of natural development. He tried to present a concept of history that was one of continuous progress gradually unfolding its meaning down the centuries. The longing for the infinite and the sublime became focused on human potentiality: the development of moral and spiritual perfection, a theme that was to become a familiar one in nineteenth-century thought. The divine is to be encountered within human history. 'The true way of worshipping God is to know and love that which is.'[4] It is easy to see why the figure of Jesus took on the contours it did in *La Vie de Jésus* when one understands the ideas shaping Renan's mind and imagination. At times it seems as though the notion of God is reduced to a metaphor for all that is best, morally and spiritually, in humanity; at other times God is seen as a kind of impersonal force within nature, driving the human race towards its own moral and spiritual destiny. Obedience to nature becomes paramount; co-operation with natural powers not only leads to self-realisation but is also identified as collaboration in the divine activity.

Though quite different from the philosophically sophisticated system of Leibniz, Renan's philosophy shares with Leibniz's theodicy – and much Enlightenment thinking – a fundamental optimism. Consequently, the concept of evil quickly becomes problematic. The existence of evil requires an explanation in this kind of universe just as much as it does in the Christian universe. Though aware of the problem, he seems not to have given it much attention and did not manage to offer a coherent theory. Having abandoned belief in a personal, transcendent God as well as belief in the devil, he seems, finally, to have offered a view in which even the most hideous crimes and agonising sufferings were nothing more than the result of a failure of individuals to co-operate intelligently with nature in the cultivation of their finer instincts.

While it is true that Renan's *La Vie de Jésus* caused an uproar when it appeared and that its author was dismissed from his professorial post at the College de France, it is evident that he had caught, in a remarkable way, the mood of his era. He dared, as Owen Chadwick comments, 'to utter what more prudent contemporaries thought but did not say'.[5] His fame grew rapidly, and what had been lost in the early debacle was restored many times over as the years passed. This indicates as much as any other phenomenon of the later part of the nineteenth century the extent to which European life and thought had become secularised. In particular, it demonstrates the way in which religion itself was being regarded – that is, as a kind of stage along the way of progress which would eventually lead human beings to a state of moral perfection.

This belief was buttressed by theories of evolution coming from the world of natural science. For most natural scientists the violence of the natural world, noted by Tennyson, and captured by him in his memorable phrase 'red in tooth and claw', was seen as the inescapable means by which the evolutionary process was forwarded. The terms 'good' and 'evil' were regarded as inappropriate in the context of their observations and conclusions, for they not only implied misplaced value-judgement, but were redolent of religion. It was not necessary to 'justify' suffering in the realm of natural science. It could be described, of course, and even explained by a theory such as that of natural selection or the survival of the fittest, but no 'justification' was required – except in so far as one could say it was the price one had to pay in the long march of progress. It was not the role of natural science to provide a theodicy; and in any case, the idea of progress had bitten deeply into Victorian sensibility, colouring nearly every theory that appeared, philosophical and scientific. Charles Darwin ended his great work on the origin of species on a triumphant note:

> Thus, from the war of nature, from famine and death, the most exalted object which we are capable of conceiving, namely the production of the higher animals, directly follows. There is grandeur in this view of life, with its several powers, having been originally breathed into a few forms or into one; and that, whilst this planet has gone cycling on according to the fixed laws of gravity, from so simple a beginning endless forms most beautiful and most wonderful have been, and are being, evolved.
>
> Hence we may look with some confidence to a secure future of equally inappreciable length. And as natural selection works solely by and for the good of each being, all corporeal and mental endowments will tend to progress to perfection.[6]

But, a hundred years later, to Dr Rieux in Camus' *The Plague*, watching the child dying of an incurable disease, this sacrifice to progress on the altar of evolution has nothing grand or beautiful about it. He may have rejected the explanation of the Church and accepted the facts of natural selection, but he sees the universe as a hateful and inhospitable place in which innocent suffering is never anything other than outrageous.

The optimistic belief in progress was not wholly victorious in nineteenth-century culture and the challenge to it came, not only from Christian theology, but more potently from an unexpected quarter. The notion of Original Sin and the concept of evil inherent in nature was to be rediscovered and reimagined in a variety of strange ways: none so exotic, provocative and influential as that which grew in the mind of another Frenchman, Charles Baudelaire (1821–67), 'the poet in whom the Romantic Muse distilled her most subtle poison'.[7] Ernest Renan was a child of Romanticism, and here was another, but his exact opposite: the movement could spawn such contradictions. Renan had taken the vaunting aspirations of Romantic poets and philosophers and had almost deified nature: to oppose and attempt to disobey the natural process was sin. Baudelaire took from Romanticism its dark apprehensions and preternatural fears and demonised nature. It was wholly evil: to obey it and to live according to its rules was to worship the Prince of Darkness. Victorian society was shocked and outraged by Baudelaire and what followed in his wake: the movement in art and letters which we know as Decadence. To all of those who were associated with the movement, evil was a central concept. Propriety and morality were mocked, the belief in progress was derided as bourgeois and banal. In their excessive attitudes and behaviour, their ostentatious cultivation of the degraded, their pursuit of perverse sensations, decadent artists and writers spat upon the conventions of European decency and rationality.

Romanticism had always had a dark side to it. In rejecting the rationality of the Enlightenment, the poets and philosophers of Romanticism not only sought the sublime and the exalted, the fine and the spiritual, but were also fascinated by the grotesque and macabre. In his book on the 'picturesque'

Christopher Hussey describes the change that overtook art and architecture:

> The picturesque phase through which each art passed, roughly between 1730 and 1830, was in each case a prelude to romanticism. It occurred at the point when an art shifted its appeal from the reason to the imagination. An art that addresses the reason, even though it does so through the eye, does not stress visual qualities. The reason wants to *know*, not to experience sensations. The romantic movement was an awakening of sensation, and, among the other sensations, that of sight required exercising.[8]

Sensation is a key concept: sensation in all its forms. Control of the body by the reason was abandoned; detachment was abhorred. In defiance of the rules of reason and detachment, every sensation became desirable, and in the most extreme forms of Romanticism the most horrible sensations – pain as well as pleasure – were avidly sought. It was even argued that pain was itself a pleasure. The genesis of this revolution lies in the eighteenth century, and Mario Praz is one of a number of scholars who have acknowledged the crucial role played by a sinister figure who died just as Romanticism was blossoming: the Marquis de Sade. Praz writes: 'Let us give Sade his due, as having been the first to expose, in all its crudity, the mechanism of *homo sensualis* . . . and admit his influence on a whole century of literature.'[9] The themes that are played later in many variations by Baudelaire and the Decadent writers (Huysmans, Swinburne etc.) are first heard in Sade. His ferocious attack on the values of the Enlightenment lay underground – and was, indeed, suppressed by political authority – for decades but surfaced half a century after his death in very different circumstances.

Sade may be seen as a kind of diabolical mirror image of William Blake. In 1793 Blake had written, 'For everything that lives is holy, life delights in life.'[10] In the previous decade Sade had turned that notion upside down in his extraordinary quasi-philosophical 'fictions', *Justine* and *Juliette*. In this world everything that lives is evil, everything is the work of a diabolical creator, and life destroys life. Evil becomes the axis of the universe; the practice of vice becomes a necessity because viciousness is the law of nature. Vice comes, therefore, to represent the active, positive force of life; virtue is the passive, negative element. (This is an extreme version of the theory that it is always easier to make wicked characters convincing in drama or novels than it is to make good ones: vice is supposed to be more interesting than virtue.) Praz comments: 'The sense of the infinite, banished from human relationships by the suppression of any spiritual meaning, takes refuge in a sort of cosmic Satanism.'[11]

But there is a curious irony in all this. Whatever the trappings of the tale (Satanic rituals and the like), the evil of this universe is actually wholly immanent: it is not, as God is not, a transcendent principle. Supernatural evil, conceived in the manner of traditional Christian theology, plays no convincing part in this scheme; it is nature which is vicious and human nature which is totally corrupt. Praz points out the peculiar result of this view of reality; if one is totally corrupt, blasphemy is no longer a possibility. Genuine blasphemy is only within the reach of those in whom there is real belief, however feeble or insecure:

> if the sadist refuses to believe in traditional religion he deprives himself of an inexhaustible source of pleasure: the pleasure of profanation or blasphemy. And then, what pleasure can be got from trampling on crucifixes, from the *faire des horreurs avec des hosties*, what savour from the Black Mass, unless he is convinced of the truth of transubstantiation?[12]

This irony was not lost on Baudelaire, a more subtle thinker than Sade, who was to shock his contemporaries as much as his eighteenth-century predecessor, by compelling them to consider the possibility that it was evil, not goodness or progress, that lay at the heart of existence; and by expressing in beautifully crafted verse a contempt for those who failed to acknowledge the truth of his observations.

The place of Charles Baudelaire in the history of literature is no longer in dispute. Execrated and feared by many in his own lifetime, he has now emerged as one of the geniuses of French poetry. The place he occupies in the history of ideas is still a matter of debate. He was certainly an artist: can he also be seen as a moralist? At first sight this seems a ludicrous proposition: a cursory reading of his work, especially *Les Fleurs du Mal (Flowers of Evil*, 1857), might suggest just the opposite: that he was actually an immoralist. In his own period many denounced him for corruption and pronounced him an immoralist, second only in his depravity to Sade himself. But times have changed and while Renan's *La Vie de Jésus* is virtually forgotten and has passed into history, *Les Fleurs du Mal* is everywhere to be seen and is received as a masterpiece. Is it simply 'for the poetry', for the technical mastery of verse form and the originality of his imagination, that Baudelaire remains an author who is continually being rediscovered? Or is there something else: the offering of a vision of the world that strikes the reader as true and alters or confirms our perception of reality?

There is, first, one clear and evident reason for Baudelaire's outrageous behaviour and the calculated squalor of his life. It was not merely to shock his bourgeois, conventional contemporaries (though it did have that intended effect too); it had a more serious purpose. It was an attempt to escape that psychological condition known well to all writers on the spiritual life: 'accidie', that profound boredom which paralyses the mind, deadens the limbs, and lays low the heart. In its worst manifestations it is close to despair, a listlessness so deep that the subject seems to be sinking into an eternal inanition. Baudelaire called it, accurately, *la maladie des moines*, for it often, paradoxically, afflicts those, like monks and nuns, whose lives are given over completely to prayer, worship and contemplation. But it is also found in the most worldly of lives and is a symptom of cynicism: 'If nothing is of any value, nothing matters; and if nothing matters, why should one bother to do anything at all?' Sensual self-indulgence is seen as one way out of this boredom: the determined, and sometimes desperate, hunt for sensations of all kinds. The end of this pursuit, when all other diversions have failed, is the cultivation of the violent and the perverse in the belief that the performance of vicious acts will give relief, will make the subject feel alive. So the poet addresses his lover:

> Those mad gowns are the emblem of
> Your many-hued soul and my love,
> O mad one who maddens *me*! you
> Whom I love, yet loathe so, too! . . .

> And thus some night, I would like,
> When the hour of pleasure doth strike,
> To your alcove in silence to creep,
> Where your body's treasures sleep,

> To chastise your joyous flesh
> And your scatheless bosom to gash,
> And to cut there before you swooned
> A wide and deep red wound.

> And – dizzy, ineffable bliss! –
> Through the lips of that new orifice
> Of a lovelier, brighter hue,
> To infuse my venom in you![13]

The spirit of Sade seems to breathe through these lines, as sensual delight turns into the desire for destruction, violent death becomes the inevitable consequence of sexual enjoyment, pleasure and pain become intertwined.

But there is something more, and different, in Baudelaire: a sense, subtly conveyed, that this need not necessarily be the only form of existence; that something has been lost, some goodness or beauty. However, such goodness or beauty as might be possible can only be perceived through the eyes of one who has the courage to acknowledge the reality of evil:

> Like immaterial air, at every turn
> The Demon haunts me, giving me no rest;
> I breathe him, swallow him, and straightaway burn
> With foul desires and everlasting lust . . .
>
> He leads me from God's eyes by his seduction,
> Breathless and broken down by weariness
> 'Mid Ennui's deep and lonely wilderness,
>
> And my confounded sight he doth appal
> With filthy raiment, open wounds, and all
> The bloody apparatus of Destruction.[14]

Religious imagery controls the poetry here and the religious sensibility is real. Baudelaire does not produce the trappings of devil worship meretriciously (as in so many lesser poets of the period) for the purpose of creating a shiver of excitement. His life and work are the products of the mind that has looked steadfastly into the abyss and recognised the darkness of the human heart and the terror of the universe. His refined poetry is used to express a horror that his contemporaries refused to admit to their less courageous imaginations. For him belief in the fundamental goodness of human nature was a lie. Original

Sin, though he seldom used this theological expression, was a primal reality; to be natural was to be enmeshed in evil, and the figure of Satan could be used as a symbol of this reality. The philosophy of progress pervading the air of the nineteenth century was derided; all talk about the triumph of morality was dismissed as the superficial babble of minds enslaved to a childish and outmoded notion of rationality. In this he stood in violent contrast to his age: the age of Darwin and Renan; the age of scientific progress and human optimism. He exposed its weaknesses and denounced its secular values by thrusting a theory of evil to the forefront of his work.

Whatever else we may find in Baudelaire, we shall find a religious sensibility seeking, however perversely, for the transcendent; embracing in his despair a kind of dualism in which the principles of good and evil are necessary to one another. As Peter Quennell writes:

> during the entire course of his life, no catastrophe, we shall find, does he dread more than a creeping paralysis of his moral feelings which should obliterate the 'two simultaneous postulates, one towards God, the other towards Satan' which (he had declared) are the indispensable companion of a man's every thought.[15]

But it was towards Satan that he turned – at least in poetry:

> Inventor's lamp and exile's staff, thou blesser
> Of scaffolds, and conspirators' confessor,
>
> Have pity, Satan, on my long affliction!
>
> Adoptive father of all those robbed of Eden,
> Whom God in black wrath banished from the Garden,
>
> Have pity, Satan, on my long affliction![16]

That is one kind of dualism: that of good and evil. There is another kind also present in Baudelaire: that of flesh and spirit:

The flesh, having been alienated from the spirit, is transformed into a goad and whip. The sensation for him loses its false independence and is returned to the stream of life, but now negatively, becoming significant because it is linked with death, sin, blasphemy. This is Logos gone mad, posing as Eros. It is extreme romanticism turned devotionally Catholic, but, in its childish egoism, enlisting under Satan.[17]

Baudelaire, like nearly all those who were later to be called Decadent, in some measure accepted a type of Manicheism and located sin in the flesh, simultaneously pleasuring it and punishing it. The extreme sensual indulgence arose, paradoxically, not out of delight in the flesh and admiration of the body, but out of distrust of the flesh and hatred of the body. 'Logos . . . posing as Eros.' There is something childish about a theology which makes the flesh more evil than the mind or the will. Though there is nothing childish about Baudelaire, there is something not quite convincingly achieved about his Satanism. In the end he cannot imagine evil in all its seriousness. He knows that it both exists and is serious, but he cannot locate it except in the flesh. It is as though he wants with all his heart to believe in Satan, but cannot; in his poetry we see souls reaching out for damnation but being unable to achieve it because they are incapable of identifying its exact place.

The comparison with Dante's *Inferno*, frequently made, is instructive here. Even if the reader does not share Dante's world-view, there can be no doubt about the convincing power in his portrayal of the damned. Dante locates sin firmly in the will, and his damned figures have deliberately and implacably willed their own fate: they oppose goodness at the very centre of their being. There is a further, and perhaps more important difference. We know what Dante's souls have lost when we read *The*

*Divine Comedy*, but we do not know what it is that Baudelaire's characters have lost. Baudelaire talked of the 'two postulates, the one towards God, the other towards Satan', but, in fact, he was unable to imagine God and unable to realise a wholly convincing vision of evil. The rebellion is against the constraints of the self-satisfied, moralistic, prurient society of nineteenth-century Europe and the religiosity of the Christian Church, not against God. Baudelaire, for all his faults, was never trivial; he perceived a reality which he expressed in ways that were both shocking and admirable, but his concept of evil lacks substance, despite the exquisite poetry in which it was realised.

Dante's world was one which believed profoundly in the reality of evil, the existence of the devil and the need for redemption. Baudelaire's world lacked such conviction. Belief in Satan was a medieval superstition, redemption a concept that had become otiose in a society which expected human nature to progress steadily towards a better future. Baudelaire longed for religion in an age which had abandoned religion, for depth of experience in a world which, it seemed to him, had become bland and smug, for ecstasy in a culture which despised everything that could not be quantified, measured and explained in terms of either morality or science. He chose to express his revulsion in a philosophy of evil because the vocabulary of goodness had become debased in the mouths of those who dominated society with their progressively humanistic religion. As T. S. Eliot remarked in his essay on Baudelaire, 'the possibility of evil or damnation is so immense a relief in a world of electoral reform, plebiscites, sex reform and dress reform, that damnation itself is an immediate form of salvation.'[18]

In the same essay Eliot quoted, without identifying it, a statement of the poet: '*La vraie civilisation n'est pas dans le gaz, ni dans la vapeur, ni dans les tables tournantes. Elle est dans la diminution des traces du peche orginel.*'[19] Quite what Baudelaire meant by 'original sin' is not clear, but his invocation of the doctrine is significant. There are no natural acts or attitudes that are intrinsically good. There are no natural acts or attitudes that are intrinsically neutral. Every act or attitude is related to a primal ground that is either good or evil, but Baudelaire's imagination, steeped as it was in Romanticism and moulded by its own historical context as well as by the peculiarities of his own temperament, could only present his readers with the ground that was evil.

His world is not our world; he died before the outbreak of the Franco-Prussian War and the siege of Paris. We have had to face the reality of evil in the recollection of the carnage of the First World War and the horror of the concentration camps. It cannot be helped if there is a fastidiousness about his sensibility that makes his diabolism seem dandified and slightly precious to a twentieth-century mind. He stood out against the complacency of his age in a way that gives his rebellion universal significance. There followed in his footsteps only smaller and sillier men: the Decadents, whose perfumed atmospheres and mannered behaviour have little energy or insight. They carry no conviction of a knowledge of real evil. This is Romanticism gone to seed; their Satanic rituals and black masses have a quality of giggling naughtiness that reminds one of little children shouting rude words in public to shock their elders. Baudelaire cannot be blamed for this; he was a genuine voice of protest in a period in which the concept of evil was being drained of meaning. He believed that only a recovery of it could enable the human being to face the reality of existence, which was wild, mysterious and frightening as well as rational, ordered and beautiful. As Eliot wrote, 'If it is true to say that the glory of man is his capacity for salvation; it is also true to say that his glory is his capacity for damnation.'[20] Life is an extreme business. In the light of the history of the twentieth century, it is not Ernest Renan's voice that sounds the prophetic note, it is Charles Baudelaire's.

# RETURNING TO EDEN:
# GOOD AS EVIL

WHETHER OR NOT Karl Barth (1886–1968) should be regarded as the greatest theologian of the twentieth century, as many have claimed, may be debated; what is probably beyond doubt is that he is the most famous. His reputation as a systematic theologian in English-speaking countries, however, was not fully established until after the Second World War when his massive work, *Die kirchliche Dogmatik* (*Church Dogmatics*), which he started in the 1930s, began to appear in an English translation. Up to this point he was known chiefly as the brilliant and devastating critic of liberal theology in the much earlier work, *Der Romerbrief* (*Epistle to the Romans*) of 1919. It was as the author of this commentary that the English poet and theologian, Charles Williams (born in the same year as Barth) knew him. In 1940 he had used several extracts from the *Epistle to the Romans* in his anthology of Christian prose and poetry, *The New Christian Year*. It is possible that what he discovered and responded to in the thought of Karl Barth was the presence of Søren Kierkegaard. Barth was profoundly indebted to the nineteenth-century Danish philosopher, and Charles Williams had found this provocative thinker so challenging and illuminating that he had successfully persuaded the Oxford University Press, for whom he worked, to publish the first translations in England of Kierkegaard's philosophy. Williams died in May

1945, and there is no evidence that he had encountered Barth's *Church Dogmatics*, nor, perhaps, that he would have found in Barth's mature writing much that would have been congenial to his own theological approach. But on the subject of evil, their thinking, improbably, bears striking resemblances as well as one notable difference. It is against the background of Barth's theology of evil – interesting, of course, in its own right – that Williams' own unique contribution to the understanding of evil will stand out more clearly.

In Part III of Volume III of the massive *Church Dogmatics*, Karl Barth turns his attention to the problem of evil. Almost immediately the thickets of language close in: what words can be found to describe the paradox with which he is confronted – the description of that which might be indescribable? The context of the presentation of a theology of evil is the doctrine of creation, and the entire section is treated under the heading, 'God and Nothingness'.[1] The term which Barth will use throughout for 'evil' is *Das Nichtige*: nothingness, nullity, the Nihil. It seems at first sight that Barth, in approaching the problem from this direction and using this vocabulary, will expound the doctrine on the foundation provided by Augustine and Thomas Aquinas: evil as negation or privation, a well-known strand of the Christian tradition. And in some senses this is true. There is the same rejection of any suggestion that evil is self-generating, independent of the power of God, existing of its own volition. In this resolute rejection of dualism nothing can be beyond the power of the Almighty; evil has no being of its own, it is essentially non-existent, a denial of the reality of what is:

> This negation of His Grace is chaos, the world which He did not choose or will, which He could not and did not create, but which, as He created the actual world, He passed over and set aside, marking and excluding it as the eternal past, the eternal

yesterday. And this is evil in the Christian sense, namely, what is alien and adverse to grace, and therefore without it. In this sense nothingness is really privation, the attempt to defraud God of His honour and right . . . Where this privation occurs, nothingness is present; and where nothingness is present this privation occurs, i.e. evil, that which is utterly inimical first to God and then to His creature.[2]

This having been said, Barth finds himself in the same dilemma as the great theologians who have gone before him: the necessity of finding a way of describing this nothingness that conveys the reality of the experience of evil. The descriptions become positive. Like the others, he cannot avoid those formulations which over and over again indicate that this pure negation is menacing, corrupting, terrifying. Absence becomes presence; nothingness invades and destroys; it seems to have existence. The fourth section of this part of the book is entitled 'The Reality of Nothingness' – a paradoxical proposition if ever there was one. So having spoken of nothingness as the 'negation of God's grace', he has to continue, 'It opposes both as an enemy, offending God and threatening His creature',[3] and later, 'nothingness is not nothing, but exists in its own curious fashion'.[4] One is left in no doubt about the terrible power of nothingness: there may be no place for the personification of evil in supernatural form, as Satan, in Barth's theology, but his sense of the almost overwhelming danger of this nothingness impresses itself indelibly on the reader's mind.

Like his predecessors, he is ambivalent on the cause of this nothingness. Why should it arise so fearsomely? Can one say that it has a cause? On the one hand, he seems to suggest that we cannot attribute the cause of evil either to God or to the human being; on the other hand, he is prepared to say that 'nothingness has its being on the left hand of God and is grounded in His non-willing.'[5] With this metaphor the causality of evil remains unresolved. Where he does differ from both Augustine and Thomas Aquinas, and also, as we shall see, from Charles Williams, is in his insistence that this nothingness can be revealed only by God's attack on it, and that it is known and recognised for what it is only in the light of its overthrow by the cross of Christ. There is only a brief discussion, in the shape of a footnote, of the myth of Eden and the Fall in this section of *Church Dogmatics*, but it is significant, for here, as elsewhere in the text, Barth's elucidation of humanity's choice of *Das Nichtige* in preference to the grace of God is remarkably similar to that of Williams: 'Hence the creature has only one good to choose, namely, that it has God for it, and that it is thus opposed by nothingness as God Himself is opposed . . .'[6]

The human creature, incomprehensibly, chooses nothingness. We find ourselves in a world of terrible absurdity: impossible possibility. The attempt is made to embrace that which cannot be embraced: nothingness. The thing cannot be – and yet is. This is the world envisaged by one of the most original minds in English theology, the world of Charles Williams.

On 15 May 1945 Charles Williams died. His tombstone in Oxford bears the simple inscription: 'Charles Walter Stansby Williams 1886–1945. Poet. Under the mercy.' It is true, he was a poet. But he was much more than a poet: from his pen flowed novels, plays, literary criticism, history, biographies – and theology. The commemoration on the gravestone is appropriate in as much as it conveys the way in which he himself hoped that he might be remembered, but it gives no clue as to where his real genius lay: in theology, in exploring and interpreting the propositions of the Christian faith with more originality and profundity than almost any of his contemporaries. This originality and profundity will be recognised, however, only by those who are willing to suspend their conventional expectations of what theology should be and to accept his belief that the art and skill of theology can be practised by the poetic imagination. He did not confuse the two, either by turning religion into aesthetics or by thinking that poetry was nothing more than a set of versified propositions, but he never believed in 'Art for Art's sake' or thought that theology was a mental discipline to be practised only by academics and seminarians. He knew and delighted in the various languages of technical theology, but he also knew that they were not for him. If he was to write theology it would be in his own way, as a poet. His prose constantly, and willingly, surrenders to the pressure of the poetic impulse, which is to reorder the movement of thought from the analytical and logical to the imaginative and the suggestive. The result is not less precision; on the contrary, it is a different kind of precision. The conclusion of an argument is not reached by syllogistic deduction from first principles or by careful weighing of the evidence, but as the inevitable climax of the mounting spirals of the imagination circling round an original proposition. The subject to which he returned over and over again, in novels, plays, poems, essays, and even literary criticism, was the problem of evil.

To most people he is known as the author of a number of strange novels, all of which revolve around issues of love and power and do so in the context of the invasion of the natural world by the supernatural. The American edition of Williams' last novel, *All Hallows' Eve*, carries an introduction by T. S. Eliot:

> To him the supernatural was perfectly natural, and the natural was also supernatural. And this peculiarity gave him that profound insight into Good and Evil, into the heights of Heaven and the depths of Hell, which provides both the immediate thrill, and the permanent message of his novels.[7]

Two misconceptions may arise in the minds of those who know only the novels: first, that Williams was a dualist of a most extreme kind, for the struggle between good and evil in these fictions is depicted as a real and terrible conflict, and supernatural as well as natural. The second is that the occult played a significant part in his understanding of evil, for there are descriptions of Satanic rituals, quasi-magical transformations of material objects and a variety of preternatural occurrences ranging from the appearance of a *doppelgänger* to the creation of a succubus. These misconceptions are caused by readers failing to recognise the genre in which Williams chose to create his fictions: they are fantasies, and they stand in a long line of 'fantastic' literature in English. The supernatural imagery is precisely that: imagery. The scenes must be received and understood at the level of metaphor. This does not make the realities they are intended to convey less real, but it does mean that the reader should not expect to experience these realities in the same way as the characters in the novels do, or that Williams expected his readers to. It is true that Williams was well acquainted with the details of some occult rituals and that he had been, for a time, a member of the occult society to which W. B. Yeats also belonged, the Order of the Golden Dawn, but he never believed that such rituals were of the substance of evil. Invocations of the devil, the performance of magical rites, occult practices of whatever kind, were neither its explanation nor its cause. He located evil firmly in the place in which both Augustine and Thomas Aquinas located it: the human will. His restrained and scholarly work on witchcraft contains a sentence in the preface which exactly indicates his own apprehension of the reality of evil:

> No one will derive any knowledge of initiation from this book; if he wishes to meet 'the tall, black man' or to find the proper way of using the Reversed Pentagram, he must rely on his own heart, which will, no doubt, be one way or other sufficient.[8]

Fascinating as the novels are, it is to his theological essays that we must turn if we wish to see the way in which Williams imagined evil.

Williams' first venture into theological territory, however, hardly addressed the subject. It was an astonishing book entitled *Outlines of Romantic Theology* and was an attempt to construct a theology based on the experience of romantic love. It remained, for various reasons, unpublished until forty years after the author's death; though themes which first made their appearance in that manuscript were taken up and developed in different ways in many of the books that followed, including his best-known theological works, *He Came Down From Heaven* (1938) and its sequel, *The Forgiveness of Sins* (1943). The two books offer, from different angles, interpretations of the central doctrines of the Christian faith: the Incarnation and the Atonement. In order to do this Williams knew he had to address the questions of sin and evil, and the second chapter of *He Came Down From Heaven* is a reading of the myth of the Fall contained in the book of Genesis.

He approaches the story from an unexpected direction: from the examination of themes that he had discussed before in two earlier works of literary criticism, *The English Poetic Mind* (1932) and *Reason and Beauty in the Poetic Mind* (1933). In both of those books Williams was examining what he called the 'Troilus experience'. How was it possible, he asked, for human beings to endure, and make sense of, the sudden reversal of fortune, the experience of the world in a completely different, and apparently contradictory mode? He focuses attention on the scene in Shakespeare's play, *Troilus and Cressida*, in which the Trojan prince Troilus is taken secretly to the Greek encampment and there sees his beloved Cressida in the arms of another man – the Greek, Diomed. Troilus is driven to the point of insanity; in the face of this treachery he begins to doubt his vision and his reason. He literally cannot believe what he is seeing:

> This she? no, this is Diomed's Cressida.
> If beauty have a soul, this is not she . . .
> If there be rule in unity itself,
> This is not she. O madness of discourse,
> That cause sets up with and against itself;
> Bi-fold authority! where reason can revolt
> Without perdition, and loss assume all reason
> Without revolt: this is, and is not, Cressida.[9]

Williams did not read this speech as a kind of hyperbolic utterance provided by the playwright to engage the audience's sympathy for the plight of the character, merely to give some idea of the depth of Troilus' feelings. He saw it as a profound philosophical statement about the way human beings experience life: those moments in which we seem to have 'double vision'; an experience of both being and not being at the same time; of something being both itself and something different; an experience of division in knowledge which comes as a sense of 'outrage' to our own perception both of the world and of ourselves.

He was to introduce this concept in a quite different context in his book on witchcraft when he tried to explain the curious interest in and urge towards magic:

The predisposition towards the idea of magic might be said to begin with a moment which seems to be of fairly common experience – the moment when it seems that anything might turn into anything else. We have grown used – and properly used – to regarding this sensation as invalid because, on the whole, things do not turn into other things except by processes which we realize, or at least so frequently that we appreciate the probability. But the occasional sensation remains . . . There is, in our human centre, a heart-gripping fear of irrational change, of perilous and malevolent change.[10]

In *Reason and Beauty in the Poetic Mind* we can see Williams beginning to extend the concept of 'outraged being' in a theological way; a way that leads directly into his treatment of sin and evil in *He Came Down From Heaven*:

> But what Shakespeare is doing from *Hamlet* onwards is twofold; he is exploring the actual schism in reason, and pressing it as much farther as he can. The perception of man is hereafter horribly doubled.[11]

The subject under discussion here is the psychological development of the creative artist, the context is the Shakespearean canon, and the vocabulary is that of literary criticism; but the movement of thought is towards a theological statement. We may or may not agree with his psychological theories in the realm of aesthetics, but it is not unreasonable to suppose that he read in the great poets with whom he was dealing a confirmation of a universal human experience: an experience of sudden unreality and internal, psychic division. This experience, the 'actual schism in reason', became the foundation of his theological exposition of the doctrine of the Fall and Original Sin in the second chapter of *He Came Down From Heaven* and elsewhere.

Williams' mind was steeped in the poetry of John Milton, but when it came to the theological implications of the Genesis myth it is not so much to *Paradise Lost* that he turns as Milton's earlier prose work, *Areopagitica*, Milton's tract on censorship and the freedom of the press. Here it immediately becomes clear that, when it came to the question of evil, Williams was not a dualist. He is simply not interested in theories of a precosmic Fall, theories about the rebel archangels and the temptation of Adam and Eve by Satan. He does, however, acknowledge the extensive influence that Milton's version of the story in *Paradise Lost* has had on English sensibility since the seventeenth century:

Our own awareness of this explanation [of evil] is generally referred to the genius of Milton, who certainly shaped it for us in great poetry and made use of it to express his own tender knowledge of the infinite capacity of man's spirit for foolish defiance of God.[12]

But, as Williams may be suggesting, Milton's own attitude to the Satanic temptation as expressed in *Paradise Lost* is highly ambivalent, even though his version of the story follows closely the Augustinian elaboration of the Genesis account in *City of God*, an account which had become traditional in Western Christianity.

It is precisely the role of Satan in the Eden myth which Williams (surprisingly, it might seem, in the light of the fantastic 'dualism' of his novels) uncompromisingly rejects here in his own interpretation of the Fall:

The popularity of the legend [the fall of Satan] has perhaps been assisted by the excuse it has seemed to offer for mankind, by the pseudo-answer it has appeared to offer to the difficulty of the philosophical imagination concerning a revolt in the good against the good [the actual schism in reason] and by the provision of a figure or figures against whom men can, on the highest principles, launch their capacities of indignant hate and romantic fear. The devil, even if he is a fact, has been an indulgence . . . [13]

This is a significant passage: it sets the tone for Williams' own reconstruction of the myth, and places certain aspects of the novels and plays in their proper perspective. Williams is freer in his handling of the Genesis myth than both Augustine and Milton for, in addition to the exclusion of the devil from Eden, the nearest he comes to the mention of a 'tempter' – a 'character' indisputably present in the original account – is a vague and passing reference to a 'serpentine subtlety'.[14] The clause 'even if he is a fact' to some degree puts a gloss on the statement, but it is not strong enough to suggest a theory about the origin of evil in which an external, demonic force can act decisively as an agent of corruption in a world in which men and women make moral choices. Throughout both *He Came Down From Heaven* and *The Forgiveness of Sins* any suggestion that there might be an eternal struggle between powers of light and darkness is rejected as unacceptable in a Christian theology. The concept of the battle against 'principalities and powers', against 'the hosts of wickedness in the heavenly places', is dismissed with a briskness that, it must be admitted, is at variance with both the witness of the New Testament and much of the Christian tradition.

Although the Church has never seen fit to pronounce dogmatically on the way in which evil is to be defined, nor the way in which the reconciliation between God and the world is accomplished when the communion between God and his creatures is disrupted by evil, it has already been seen that certain theories have captured the Christian imagination and governed the thinking of writers and teachers since the first century. Among the most prominent has been the image of victory. Gustav Aulen, in his critical survey of the history of the theme, *Christus Victor*, argues persuasively for its centrality not only in the theology of the New Testament, but also in the patristic expositions of both Eastern and Western Christendom:

> the classic idea [victory] is the dominant view of the Western as of the Eastern fathers. We find it in Ambrose, pseudo-Ambrose, Augustine, Leo the Great, Caeserius of Arles, Faustus of Rhegium, and Gregory the Great.[15]

Though we may doubt that the idea is quite as dominant as Aulen would have us believe, the pervasiveness and ubiquity of the idea is undeniable. The image of victory has embedded itself in the devotion, the liturgy, the theology and the art of the Church since the patristic era. Yet Williams resolutely excluded the idea from his own interpretation of the doctrine of Atonement. His 'monistic' interpretation of the universe, with its scepticism about the reality and the power of supernatural evil, gives his doctrine of the Atonement its distinctive and unusual character. If evil has no supernatural origin, where and how does it arise and how is it undone?

It might be argued that his attitude may be seen as part of the general trend which we have already examined: the tendency in the West since the seventeenth century towards a decline in belief in the supernatural and the inexorable secularisation of culture. Aulen writes of this change in the religious climate:

> Dualism was not popular with the Liberal Protestant theology of the eighteenth and nineteenth centuries; but the classic idea of the Atonement is dualistic and dramatic: it depicts the drama of the Atonement against a dualistic background. If Dualism is eliminated, it is impossible to go on thinking of the existence of powers hostile to God, and the basis of the classic view has been dissolved away. Now, the leading theology from the time of the Enlightenment to the nineteenth century lay under the influence of an idealistic metaphysic, and was definitely monistic and evolutionary.[16]

By no stretch of the imagination could Williams be called a Liberal Protestant – he was a thoroughgoing 'supernaturalist'. But he was also, like them, a thoroughgoing 'monist', and would not admit to his system of thought the possibility of a world under the power of any agency other than God.

In chapter 7 of *He Came Down From Heaven* he propounds his belief with startling clarity and sublime confidence:

> There is no split second of the unutterable horror and misery of the world that he did not foresee (to use the uselessness of

that language) when he created; no torment of children, no
obstinacy of social wickedness, no starvation of the innocent,
no prolonged and deliberate cruelty, which he did not know . . .
The First Cause cannot escape being the First Cause . . . The
pious have been — as they always are — too anxious to excuse
him . . . [17]

This rejection of dualism is developed further in the later essay,
*The Cross* (1943), which approaches the person and work of
Christ from another angle. It can be seen there that he is
prepared to drive his argument to its logical conclusion: if there
is evil in the world, God must be held responsible for it and
answer to humankind for it. His understanding of Atonement
is focused, not on victory over evil, but on the way in which
it might be possible to reconcile two apparently contradictory
notions: God's love and God's justice. Familiar territory, but
Williams' attempt differs in interesting ways from those of his
predecessors in the Christian tradition. The very language of
the passage just quoted is sufficient evidence of the distinction
between the theology of Williams and that of the Liberal Prot-
estants. He never loses sight of the misery and darkness of
human existence and is concerned to draw our attention to sin
and evil with as much vigour as Baudelaire. Furthermore, his
is neither an idealist metaphysic nor a confident evolutionary
theory. The refusal of dualism has its roots in his reading of the
Genesis story, a reading which could be called eccentric, even
original, in the relation it has to the interpretation of the Fall
story through nineteen hundred years of Christian history.

In his book, *The Problem of Pain*, C. S. Lewis correctly points
to the curiously limited way in which the Genesis account has
generally been interpreted by the teachers of the Christian
tradition:

The story in Genesis is a story (full of the deepest suggestion)
about a magic apple of knowledge: but in the developed doctrine

the inherent magic of the apple has quite dropped out of sight, and the story is simply one of disobedience . . . I therefore do not doubt that the version which emphasises the magic apple, and brings together the tree of life and knowledge, contains a deeper and subtler truth than the version which makes the apple simply and solely a pledge of obedience.[18]

Williams' reading of the story concentrates on the 'magic apple' and is a striking example of the way in which the poetic imagination can illuminate areas that have been left dark by the more abstract philosophical mind. His attempt to reach those 'deeper and subtler truths' may have been influenced by a phrase that occurs in Milton's *Areopagitica*. The moral content of the myth – disobedience to the divine command – is not entirely dismissed or ignored, but the interpretation revolves around the question of knowledge. He sets aside judgement of the moral question of whether Adam and Eve should or should not have obeyed the Lord in favour of an examination of the symbolism of the act itself. The central symbol is the tree of the knowledge of good and evil: it is towards this that Adam and Eve reach and from this that they take and eat.

In his brief reference to the Fall in *Areopagitica* Milton remarks:

it was from out the rinde of one apple tasted, that the knowledge of good and evill as two twins cleaving together leapt forth into the World. And perhaps this is that doom which Adam fell into of knowing good and evill, that is of knowing good by evill.[19]

That last phrase must have been known to Williams, though not, perhaps consciously remembered, for he makes no reference to *Areopagitica* here, and proceeds to offer an interpretation of the theology of the Genesis myth that is quite different from, and more sophisticated than Milton's. Nonetheless, one cannot help noticing in chapter 2 of *He Came Down From Heaven* something that reads like an elaborate gloss on Milton's words. Milton's argument is relatively simple: if one wishes to know what good is, one must also be able to recognise evil; if one is unaware of the distinction between good and evil one will not be free to choose between the two. In order to preserve the doctrine of the freedom of the will Milton makes the opposite of good – evil – a necessary part of human experience: one could not know the one without the other. The acquisition of the knowledge of evil becomes a necessary part of the development of the human psyche: one would not be free unless one knew evil. It is a strangely benign view of evil. This is not the way the story is construed by Williams.

Like Milton, he sees that the myth, with the tree of the knowledge of good and evil as its symbolic centre, is about freedom and knowledge, but, unlike Milton, he does not make evil necessary for the knowledge of good. His way of paraphrasing and commenting on the simple biblical statement, 'their eyes were opened' (Gen. 3:7) is to assert that 'all difference consists in *the mode* of knowledge' (my italics):

> They knew good; they wished to know good and evil. Since there was not – since there never has been and never will be – anything but the good to know, they knew good as antagonism. All difference consists in the mode of knowledge.[20]

The forms and structures of existence, human nature and the total environment – that is, the 'facts' of creation – remain unchanged; but in the eating of the fruit Adam and Eve's perception and understanding of those facts undergo a radical reversal. The world remains good, it remains itself, but human nature is changed. It no longer has the capacity for recognising reality as good because it has desired to know something that cannot be known, to know existence in a mode that cannot be known. This is the meaning of the paradoxical assertion that

Adam and Eve wished to know the good 'as evil'. (It is interesting to note that where Milton had written 'to know good *by* evill', Williams has written 'to know good *as* evil'.) The 'opening' of human eyes results not in an increase in knowledge, as in Milton's simpler interpretation, but in knowledge in another mode: negativity, the absence of good. There can be no more facts to know: Adam and Eve are intent on knowing something that they cannot, by definition, know – namely, the absence of fact, which is why Williams calls the Eden myth a tale of impossibility. Humanity's story in Eden becomes a tragic tale of destruction by illusion: trusting in the lie that it is possible to know nothing, the absence of what is, and still remain human. But Adam and Eve, through the terrible grace of God, do not die, nor do they become something other than human; they are driven from the garden. However, the price of their being sustained in existence is the introduction into the human pysche of a horrible division: good is now known as evil. Good and its absence are, from this point on, to be known simultaneously.

Williams arrived at this interpretation by his conviction that the central teaching of the orthodox tradition on the nature of evil was correct. From Augustine onwards evil was, as we have already seen, defined in negative terms, as *privatio boni*, the absence of good. Augustine is one of the two thinkers to whom Williams makes direct reference in this section of *He Came Down From Heaven*. The other is Thomas Aquinas, and it is interesting to see that it is Thomas whom he uses to develop his own distinctive exposition of the problem of evil. He realises that he is faced with a paradox. If evil is the absence of good, essentially non-existent, how can it be possible for the human creature to have knowledge of that which by definition has no real being? He tries to solve the problem by resorting to Thomas' distinction between knowledge that is proper to God and knowledge that belongs to man. The knowledge possessed by the divine being is a knowledge which can apprehend possibility as well as actuality, and Williams directs his readers to the fifteenth question of the *Summa Theologica*, where the medieval theologian draws a distinction between knowledge 'by vision' and knowledge by 'simple intelligence'. It is possible, according to Thomas, for God to know absence or privation without causing it. It is not possible for the human being to know in this way: that is the condition of creation. The fundamental premise of Thomas' treatise *On Creation* is that all beings apart from God are not their own being, but are beings 'by participation', and this implies different kinds of knowledge. In the third article of the forty-fifth question the premise is expounded in the following way: 'But in God relation to the creature is not a real relation, but a relation of reason; whereas the relation of the creature to God is a real relation.'

On the basis of this proposition Williams argues that the promise of the serpent to Eve that she and Adam would be 'as gods' if they ate of the fruit of the tree of the knowledge of good and evil was a lie. Human being and divine being differ in the mode of knowing: it is impossible for human creatures to possess purely 'intellectual' knowledge – that is, knowledge 'by simple intelligence'. Human knowledge is existential: we cannot have knowledge that does not affect being. To know is to experience. So to know the absence of good is to be deprived of the experience of good.

Williams asks the question, 'What does it mean, in existential terms, to experience the absence of good? If it is not simply death, what then is is?' His answer is the 'Troilus experience', an experience he had first imagined and then translated into the language of theology. It is the experience of extreme alienation in which the features of creation alter under our gaze:

> one may be with a friend, and a terror will take one even while his admirable voice is speaking: one will be with a lover and the hand will become a different and terrifying thing, moving in

one's own like a malicious intruder, too real for anything but fear.[21]

This is the 'unutterable schism in reason'; existence known as antagonism, the experience of 'knowing good as evil'. Hell is heaven's love and joy known in a different mode: as pain and horror. For Williams, one of the most perplexing aspects of the situation is why God should choose to maintain his creation in existence at all, given that this is an existence in which good is known as evil and fact is experienced as antagonism. It is a version of the complaint of Job, and Williams addresses the question in all its mystery in his essay on the cross.

Since it was written in the middle of the confusion and anxieties of the Second World War, there can be little doubt that his awareness of the sufferings and slaughter of the conflict contributed to the dark tone of the essay. Referring early to our freedom to choose either good or evil, he remarks:

> It is not credible that a finite choice ought to result in an infinite distress: or rather let it be said that, although credible, it is not tolerable (to us) that the Creator should deliberately maintain and sustain His created universe in a state of infinite distress as a result of that choice. No doubt it is possible to Him.[22]

It is a sombre and even angry piece, turning upon the notion of the justice of God in relation to the suffering of the universe – the dilemma of Dr Rieux. Once again the rejection of dualism is unequivocal. Responsibility for the suffering cannot be laid at the feet of the devil; there is no supernatural power opposed to God that can be blamed for evil, either physical or moral, in the world. It arises out of the free choice of human beings. However, human beings are not responsible for their freedom; that arises out of the will of the source of all joy, which, we are told by our Christian faith, is God:

> Our distress then is no doubt our gratuitous choice, but it is

also His. He could have willed us not to be after the Fall. He did not. Now the distress of the creation is so vehement and prolonged, so tortuous and torturing, that even naturally it is revolting to our sense of justice, much more supernaturally.[23]

Here is a modern Job questioning God's justice. The ancient Job received an answer to his complaint which silenced him: a theophany, a revelation of God's splendour and power. The modern Job also receives a theophany, but one as utterly unlike the first as could be imagined, a revelation of God's apparent weakness and humility. He does not, he cannot, by a *fiat*, simply declare evil not to be. The theophany comes in the shape of the crucified Lord: the cross. This does not provide, in terms of philosophical analysis, the explanation or the justification of innocent suffering, but, says Williams, it does 'enable us to use the word "justice" without shame'.[24] In the death of Christ, the Son of God, 'He deigned to endure the justice He decreed.'[25] Does this have an effect on the nature of the suffering? Can evil be undone? Can our mode of knowledge be changed? To all these questions Williams gives an affirmative answer. The rest of the essay, like the rest of the earlier book, *He Came Down From Heaven*, is devoted to the means by which this is achieved, the explication of the meaning of the doctrine of the Incarnation. The flesh-taking of the Son of God is seen as the only way in which the reversal of the 'actual schism in reason' can be accomplished. Good had become known as evil; evil must now become known as good.

He submitted in our stead to the full results of the Law which is He. We may believe He was generous if we know that He was just. By that central substitution, which was the thing added by the cross to the Incarnation, He became everywhere the centre of, and everywhere He energized and reaffirmed, all our substitutions and exchanges. He took what remained, after the Fall, of the torn web of humanity in all times and in all places, and not so much by a miracle of healing as by a growth within it made it whole. Supernaturally He renewed our proper nature.[26]

When his friend and biographer, Alice Mary Hadfield, told him that she was about to read Dante's *Divine Comedy* he advised her to begin, not with the first part, *Inferno*, but with the last, *Paradiso*. By doing that she would be enthralled by the sensations of hell, but would see where the journey ended. The intention of *Inferno* could only be understood in the light of what was contained in *Paradiso*. The final note was joy. The modern mind, he argued, was unaccustomed to such a notion and did not take the promise of it seriously. The medieval poet would not have the reader dwell in the pit of darkness and the punishment for sin; his or her mind should be set on the sight of God. Evil did not define the good, good defined the evil; hell could tell us nothing about heaven, but heaven could tell us all about hell. So it was with Williams himself. Few people have penetrated so deeply into the mystery of iniquity as he did, yet, like Dante, implicit in all he wrote was the sense that far more important than this mystery was the mystery of God, that evil should only be approached from the side of goodness. In this he stands squarely in the tradition of orthodox theology, and perhaps he is saying neither more nor less than the masters upon whom he depended, Augustine and Aquinas. But he said it differently, and illuminated what was already known from them and others by the singular power of his imagination.

# AFTERWORD

*Once the human race has an experience which it has found to be in part authentic, it does not let it go.*

Owen Chadwick[1]

IN A UNIVERSE without God how is it possible to talk about evil? Friedrich Nietzsche announced confidently in 1882 in *The Gay Science* that God was dead. Precisely what he meant by this startling proclamation is not easy to determine. That it was intended to be a metaphysical statement about the existence, or rather the non-existence, of a supernatural being may, perhaps, be doubted. What is beyond dispute is that in its coded way, the statement was an acute piece of sociological analysis. Nietzsche had observed what was happening in European society in the latter part of the nineteenth century and had noted that the concept of God had generally become so etiolated that the Christian religion could no longer be regarded as having a significant role to play in the development of culture. This is the process that came to be called secularisation: a loosening of the hold of religious belief and practice on the minds and hearts of the greater part of the population; and with this displacement of religion came 'a freeing of the sciences, of learning, of the arts, from their theological origins or theological bias'.[2] In his book of 1888, *Beyond Good and Evil*, Nietzsche followed up his proposition about the death of God with a renunciation of the categories of thought provided by the Judaeo-Christian tradition. It is true that his own philosophy, for all its brilliance, did not commend itself to many of his contemporaries, but he saw the point about the nature of the language in which those categories, good and evil, were expressed with as much clarity as Charles Baudelaire, and far more clearly than most of those who were eager to denounce his writings as the ravings of a lunatic. But whereas Baudelaire believed he could pierce the carapace of bourgeois humanism by the deployment of religious language in metaphor and symbol, Nietzsche sensed that the terms were so closely woven into the structure of orthodox religious sensibility that some new linguistic coinage might be needed.

Despite the process of the secularisation of Western culture, the language of that culture remains remarkably resistant to the pressures of secularisation. It seems as though there is an inability or an unwillingness, conscious or unconscious, to abandon a vocabulary that is implicitly religious in its connotations; though perhaps it is simply too soon for us to be sure that at some future point the human race will not discard the words that carry this baggage as the shards of an obsolete mode of existence. Despite the fact that words can change meanings and be understood in new ways, I doubt that those which refer explicitly to the supernatural or the transcendent, of which there are still many in everyday usage, can ever be entirely 'desacralised', so radically reinterpreted that they lose altogether their point of reference. The word 'evil' is a peculiarly interesting example. It does not refer explicitly to God or the supernatural, yet its meaning has been so strongly determined by religious usage that it is extremely difficult for even the most secular of modern philosophers to write about it in a way that entirely avoids religious connotations. The fascination of the problem of evil is still as strongly present to the philosophical mind as it has ever been. There is, of course, and has been for a long time, a determined effort on the part of some thinkers to resolve issues of theology into issues of morality; to try to replace concepts of good and evil with concepts of right and wrong; to use words from the vocabulary of ethical discourse which do not bear the imprint of their theological origins in nearly so obvious a way.

It was precisely in opposition to this tendency, in evidence throughout the nineteenth century, that a person like Charles Baudelaire reacted so shockingly. The world which he saw coming into being was one which was both shallow and boring, and, for him, only the recovery of some profound notion of evil could rescue it from its tedious superficiality. But he stands an isolated, prophetic figure in the landscape of his own age, unable to persuade his contemporaries of the truth of his vision of human life and the world it inhabited, for forces were at work which greatly encouraged the secular interpretation of culture and made the Western mind even less sympathetic to the notion of radical evil. Among the most powerful were those which came from the direction of the natural sciences. The influence of Charles Darwin's work on natural selection is immense and continuing. Whatever Darwin himself may have believed about religion and morality, neither religion nor morality would seem to have a place in the descriptions of the natural order provided by modern convinced 'Darwinians'. To some radical followers of Darwin it is time for all notions of good and evil, as they have been understood and preserved in religious tradition, to be set aside as concepts that have become otiose and irrelevant to a true and proper interpretation of the natural world. Value judgements, such as those offered by words like 'good' and 'evil', cannot be made when addressing the facts of nature.

Richard Dawkins in his combative book, *River Out of Eden*, tries to demonstrate just how futile it can be to employ these words if one is adopting a world-view, like his, which resolutely excludes the concept of God from the universe. He argues that one of the hardest lessons for human beings to learn is that

> nature is not cruel, only pitilessly indifferent ... We cannot admit that things might be neither good nor evil, neither kind nor cruel, but simply callous – indifferent to suffering, lacking all purpose.[3]

He observes tartly that we human beings are always asking 'Why?' questions, that we 'have purpose on the brain'. The question posed down the centuries – 'Why? Why all this suffering? Why am I here?' – all the way from Job to Camus, is not a question that is proper to ask of the universe that we know, for there can be no reply. Such a question makes presuppositions about moral issues such as order and justice, that cannot be read into, or out of, the facts of existence as they can be ascertained by the rules of Darwinian science. Dawkins' river is the river of DNA, relentlessly 'flowing and branching through geological time':

> In a universe of blind physical force and genetic replication, some people are going to get hurt, other people are going to get lucky, and you won't find any rhyme or reason in it, nor any justice. The universe we observe has precisely the properties we should expect if there is, at bottom, no design, no purpose, no evil and no good, nothing but blind, pitiless indifference.[4]

This is not to say that the author is blind or heartless, impervious to the miseries of humankind, but merely that he arrives at the conclusion that Nietzsche had reached in quite another context a century ago: the irreducibly religious connotations of these words, 'good' and 'evil', and that it is misguided to introduce the concepts into the sphere of biology.

It is difficult for us, conditioned as we are by the assumptions of our own scientific age, not to find this argument persuasive; and I should suppose that, despite the attempts of fundamentalist

Christians and Creationist theorists who try to argue for the basic veracity of the biblical accounts of creation, most people, to a greater or lesser degree, are convinced by Darwin's findings and conclusions. But how far can this point of view be carried? Can a radical Darwinism be used as a tool for interpreting the whole of reality, for making sense of every human experience? Or is 'making sense' an activity too closely akin to the notion of purpose to be permitted into our discourse? Will there never again be that sense of outrage expressed by the book of Job? Or that sense of despair found in the writings of Camus? Of course, Job's anger, sorrow and bewilderment spring from his belief in God and his notion of the moral universe established by that God. Camus' universe is as empty of divinity as Dawkins', but he reacts very differently to what he perceives to be this godless existence. He comes to a similar conclusion: that the universe is blind and indifferent to the sufferings of human beings, but he feels impelled to ask 'Why? What is the purpose?' The difference is that the 'Why' question is as central for Camus as it is irrelevant for Dawkins. It is from the paradox of having to ask the 'Why?' question – 'Why is this tiny child dying in such agony?' – and, at the same time, knowing that it cannot be answered, that Camus' philosophy grows. Camus accepts the fact of the indifference of the universe – and despairs. This is the source of the human experience of alienation; what he called 'our miserable and magnificent existence'. The human being is defined as human by the paradox embodied in the necessity of being compelled to pose a question that cannot be answered. Even though it is not a question that can be answered, it is a question that must be asked. And if the Darwinian scientist should say that this is absurd, he or she would be exactly right: life is absurd. Innocent suffering, all physical evil, makes the point.

It is worth noting that Richard Dawkins in *River Out of Eden* allows himself the use of the word 'tragic' from time to time.

He refers to the tragic death of Woody Guthrie from Huntington's chorea and the tragedy of the crash of a bus of schoolchildren. Why, we may ask, should anything be regarded as tragic in an indifferent universe? The idea of tragedy implies pity and protest, and can only arise in a context in which one feels that the moral order has been overthrown by the calamitous event. We complain that this event which has happened ought not to have happened; if there is no protest there is not tragedy, only sadness. Furthermore, its meaning occurs in the interplay between freedom and determination: between the free choice of human beings and the determined framework within which this choice is exercised. It implies a world in which events might have been different had different decisions been made. It disappears where no such possibility exists, where things just are, where another outcome to the situation cannot be envisaged. Events in the non-human world of nature cannot be called tragic because that world is one which is determined and cannot be other than it is, nor can the inhabitants of that world imagine it other than it is. Human existence becomes tragic because it is an existence that is caught between freedom and destiny – unless one is to suppose that the process of DNA *determines* all reality. Human beings exercise their choices in the tension between a world that is given and a world that can be imagined and chosen. As Helen Gardner says, 'Its matter is made up of what men do and what men suffer. Its pattern is woven out of the action and the suffering.'[5]

We can envisage a world other than the one we inhabit; a life which is characterised, for instance, by justice, love and peace. We may not often achieve these states either in private or public, but we can imagine the possibility of these states and raise the voice of protest when the possibility is denied. The great artists of Western culture have made this theme, tragedy, a recurrent preoccupation of our culture, and the Christian Church has tried to deal with this awareness in all that it has taught. The concept of tragedy cannot be separated from the notion of freedom, and the notion of freedom is inseparable from the choice of good or evil. Perhaps, to the radical followers of Darwin, it is merely a matter of subjective perception. We perceive life as tragic and unhappy only because, in our feebleness and wilful ignorance, we are unable to face the truth about existence, which is that it is morally neutral.

The discoveries of natural science force us, if we are honest, to return to the myth of Eden and re-examine it; to look again at those traditional interpretations which have seen a causal link between the Fall of Adam and Eve and the entry of death and suffering into the world. Modern zoology leads us to suppose that death and sickness, earthquakes and floods, have always been part of the structure of the planet; that there is no evidence for a historical 'transition' from a state of Edenic perfection in which there was neither death nor suffering to a 'fallen' state in which life is marked by pain and mortality. It was only through a long process of evolution that self-conscious life appeared; the kind of life to which we have given the name 'human being'. With this self-consciousness there appeared also that which we call freedom and the knowledge that mankind is both part of nature and above nature: the source of the tragic sense. Acceptance of a theory of evolution need not evacuate the myth of its potency, but it does require us to read it differently and see the relation between physical evil and moral evil (murder, cruelty, hatred, envy etc.) in a different way. It will require us to view pain and death not as evil and outrageous, arising out of some act in the distant past, but as plain and inescapable facts of biological existence. Physical and moral evil become separated. It could be argued, moreover, that the very awareness and acceptance of pain and suffering in the natural order – that is, in the physical structure of our own being – opens up the arena in which we, as self-conscious creatures, will exercise our freedom – and most particularly our freedom to love. The transcendence of our determination as purely natural beings, subject to the laws that govern all natural processes, will be accomplished not by regarding those laws as evil but by using those processes as occasions for love. The tragic person is the individual who is destroyed by the implacable laws of the universe and cannot see how they can be used as occasions of love. The character of this love would be such that the most that physical evil (and perhaps moral evil) could do to such a love would be to provide it with fresh opportunities for loving.

While the Genesis myth may not be a story of the way in which physical ills became part of natural existence, it may still be a story of an evil that is deliberately chosen by human nature from the heart of human freedom; and moral evil remains, as mysterious and frightening as ever. This new self-consciousness opens not only upon possibilities for happiness and creativity, but also upon the possibility of horror in the chasm of nothingness that is the contradiction of life in the good. In this attempt to embrace nothingness, to know the good as evil, there will be no depth of depravity or savagery to which the human being cannot sink. We shall not be able to escape responsibility; to take refuge in the position of saying that the cruel and malicious acts we commit are only the result of an irresistible force of nature. The myth is a story both about our origin and our destiny and also about our freedom and responsibility. It still has the power to unlock those terrors of our freedom that we try to forget or explain away. It opens the door of the imagination to explore and express that apprehension of a reality which has always troubled mankind. No amount of analysis by philosophers, speculation by theologians or deduction by scientists, however convincing, will make us so deeply aware of that reality. Such truths can only be reached by way of the imagination.

# NOTES

## Foreword

1. 'Art and Society', in John and Jane Dillenberger (eds.), *On Art and Architecture* (New York, Crossroad, 1989), p. 15.

## Chapter 1: The problem posed: A myth of origins

1. Albert Camus, *The Plague*, trans. Stuart Gilbert (London, Penguin Books, 1982), p. 78.
2. Ibid., p. 80.
3. Ibid., p. 107.
4. Ibid., p. 176.
5. Hesiod, *Works and Days*, trans. Dorothea Wender (London, Penguin Books, 1976), lines 89–90.
6. Joseph Campbell, *The Masks of God: Primitive Mythology* (London, Secker & Warburg, 1959), p. 4.
7. Northrop Frye, *Creation and Recreation* (University of Toronto Press, 1980), p. 29.
8. James Barr, *The Garden of Eden & the Hope of Immortality* (London, SCM Press, 1992), p. 4.

## Chapter 2: Job's complaint: The appearance of Satan

1. Carl Gustav Jung, *Memories, Dreams, Reflections*, trans. Richard and Clara Winston (London, Fount, 1978), p. 373.
2. *King Lear*, Act IV, Scene I.

3. James Wood, *Job and the Human Situation* (London, Geoffrey Bles, 1966), p. 120.

## Chapter 3: 'I saw Satan fall like lightning'

1. Tertullian, *Apology*, trans. C. Dodgson, *Tertullian* Vol. I, *Apology* (Oxford, OUP, 1842), p. 53.
2. C. S. Lewis, *Mere Christianity* (London, Fontana, 1952), p. 47.
3. Rudolf Bultmann, *Jesus Christ and Mythology* (London, SCM, 1960), p. 15.
4. Peter Vardy, *The Puzzle of Evil* (London, Fount, 1992), p. 170.

## Chapter 4: Does a shadow exist?

1. Augustine in *Rebecca West: A Celebration* (London, Penguin, 1978), p. 164.
2. Ibid., p. 210.
3. Augustine, *Confessions*, trans. H. Chadwick (Oxford University Press, 1991).
4. G. R. Evans, *Augustine on Evil* (Cambridge University Press, 1982), p. 31.
5. Augustine in *Rebecca West: A Celebration*, op. cit. p. 187.
6. John Burnaby, *Amor Dei* (London, Hodder & Stoughton, 1938), p. 200.
7. Augustine, *City of God*, trans. H. Bettenson, ed. D. Knowles (London, Penguin, 1972), XX.7, 14.
8. Evans, op. cit., p. 98.
9. *The City of God*, op. cit., p. 432.
10. Ibid., p. 871.

## Chapter 5: Medieval transformations

1. C. S. Lewis, *The Allegory of Love* (Oxford, Oxford University Press, 1958), p. 14.
2. 'Medieval Man' in Jacques Le Goff (ed.), *The Medieval World*, trans. Lydia G. Cochrane (London, Collins & Brown, 1990), pp. 6–7.
3. Charles Williams, *Witchcraft* (Oxford, Oxford University Press, 1942), pp. 73–4.

4. William Neil, *The Christian Faith in Art* (London, Hodder & Stoughton, 1966), pp. 120–21.
5. Thomas Aquinas, *Summa contra Gentiles*, trans. Vernon J. Bourke (Garden City, N.Y., Doubleday Image Books, 1956), Book III, Part 1, pp. 48–9.
6. Thomas Aquinas, *Summa Theologica*, trans. Fathers of the English Dominican Province, Part I, Second Number, Question 49 (London, R. T. Washbourne, 1912), pp. 275–6.
7. Dante, *The Inferno*, trans. C. S. Singleton (Princeton, Princeton University Press, 1970), Canto I, lines 1–6.
8. Ibid., Canto III, lines 1–9.
9. Dorothy L. Sayers, Introduction to *The Divine Comedy, Hell* (London, Penguin), pp. 10–11.
10. Dorothy L. Sayers, *The Poetry of Search and the Poetry of Statement* (London, Gollancz, 1963), pp. 240–41.

## Chapter 6: The return of Satan: 'Evil be thou my good'

1. William Blake, *The Marriage of Heaven and Hell*, 1790.
2. A. N. Wilson, *The Life of John Milton* (Oxford, Oxford University Press, 1984), p. 192.
3. *Paradise Lost*, Book I, lines 1–6, 22–6.
4. Wilson, op. cit., p. 213.
5. *Paradise Lost*, Book I, lines 249–55.
6. Ibid., Book IV, lines 40–41.
7. Maurice Bowra, 'Milton and the Destiny of Man' in *From Virgil to Milton* (London, Macmillan, 1945), p. 220.
8. *Paradise Lost*, Book IV, lines 64–78.
9. Ibid., Book IV, lines 108–13.
10. C. S. Lewis, Preface to *Paradise Lost* (Oxford University Press, 1963), p. 99.
11. C. A. Patrides (ed.), *John Milton: Selected Prose* (London, Penguin, 1974), p. 212.
12. Bowra, op. cit., p. 222.
13. *Paradise Lost*, Book I, lines 254–5.

## *Chapter* 7: **Everything for the best**

1.  Voltaire, *Candide*, trans. John Butt (London, Penguin, 1947), p. 20.
2.  Ibid., p. 33.
3.  Ibid., p. 35.
4.  Richard S. Westfall, *Science and Religion in Seventeenth-Century England* (New Haven, Yale University Press, 1958), p. 200.
5.  William Law, *A Serious Call to a Holy and Devout Life*, The Temple Classics (London, J. M. Dent, 1905), pp. 370–71.
6.  A. D. Nuttall (ed.), Preface, *Pope's 'Essay on Man'* (London, George Allen & Unwin, 1984).
7.  Pope, *Essay on Man*, Epistle I, line 16.
8.  Ibid., Epistle I, line 289.
9.  Ibid., Epistle I, line 394.
10. Ibid., Epistle I, line 70.
11. Nuttall, op. cit., p. 203.

## *Chapter* 8: **Evil romanticised: The lure of depravity**

1.  Owen Chadwick, *The Secularization of the European Mind in the Nineteenth Century* (Cambridge, Cambridge University Press, 1985), p. 219.
2.  B. M. G. Reardon, *Religion in an Age of Romanticism* (Cambridge, Cambridge University Press, 1985), p. 237.
3.  Ibid., p. 238.
4.  Ibid., p. 249.
5.  Chadwick, op. cit., p. 218.
6.  Charles Darwin, *On the Origin of Species*, ed. J. W. Burrow (London, Penguin Classics, 1985), p. 459–60. The text is that of the first edition, 1859.
7.  Mario Praz, *The Romantic Agony*, trans. A. Davidson (Oxford, Oxford University Press, 1954), p. 40.
8.  Christopher Hussey, *The Picturesque* (London, Cassell, 1927), p. 4.
9.  Praz, op. cit., p. x.
10. William Blake, *America*, line 71.
11. Praz, op. cit., p. 105.
12. Ibid., p. 107.
13. Charles Baudelaire, 'To Her Who is Too Merry', *Les Fleurs du Mal*, trans. Alan Conder (London, Cassell, 1952), pp. 224–5.

14. Baudelaire, 'Destruction', *Le Fleurs du Mal*, op. cit., p. 184.
15. Peter Quennell, *Baudelaire and the Symbolists* (London, Weidenfeld & Nicholson, 1954), p. 31.
16. Baudelaire, 'The Litanies of Satan', *Les Fleurs du Mal*, op. cit., p. 203.
17. J. B. Priestley, *Literature and Western Man* (London, Sphere Books, 1980), p. 223.
18. T. S. Eliot, 'Baudelaire', *Selected Essays* (London, Faber & Faber, 1951), p. 427.
19. Ibid., p. 430.
20. Ibid., p. 429.

## *Chapter 9*: Returning to Eden: Good as evil

1. Karl Barth, *Church Dogmatics*, Authorised English Translation (Edinburgh, T. & T. Clark, 1960).
2. Ibid., pp. 353–4.
3. Ibid., p. 354.
4. Ibid., p. 360.
5. Ibid., p. 360.
6. Ibid., p. 359.
7. Charles Williams, *All Hallows' Eve* (Grand Rapids, USA, William B. Eerdmans, 1981), p. xi.
8. Williams, *Witchcraft* (Wellingborough, Aquarian Press, 1980), p. xix.
9. William Shakespeare, *Troilus and Cressida*, Act V, Scene II.
10. Williams, *Witchcraft*, op. cit., p. 77.
11. Williams, *Reason and Beauty in the Poetic Mind* (London, Oxford University Press, 1933), p. 4.
12. Williams, *He Came Down From Heaven* (London, Faber & Faber, 1938), p. 5.
13. Ibid., p. 18.
14. Ibid., p. 20.
15. Gustav Aulen, *Christus Victor*, trans. A. G. Herbert (London, SPCK, 1931), p. 55.
16. Ibid., p. 27.
17. Williams, *He Came Down From Heaven*, op. cit., p. 99.
18. C. S. Lewis, *The Problem of Pain* (London, Fontana, 1957), pp. 59–60.
19. John Milton, *Areopagitica* in C. A. Patrides (ed.), *John Milton: Selected Prose* (London, Penguin, 1974), p. 213.

20. Williams, *He Came Down From Heaven*, op. cit., p. 21.
21. Williams, *Witchcraft*, op. cit., p. 77.
22. Williams, *The Image of the City and Other Essays*, selected by Anne Ridler (Oxford, Oxford University Press, 1958), p. 131.
23. Ibid., p. 132.
24. Ibid., p. 132.
25. Ibid., p. 132.
26. Ibid., p. 138.

## Afterword

1. Owen Chadwick, *The Secularization of the European Mind in the Nineteenth Century* (Cambridge University Press, 1985), p. 265.
2. Ibid., p. 264.
3. Richard Dawkins, *River Out of Eden: A Darwinian View of Life* (London, Weidenfeld & Nicholson, 1995), p. 96.
4. Ibid., p. 133.
5. Helen Gardner, *Religion and Literature* (London, Faber & Faber, 1971), p. 25.

# INDEX

*In most cases where a page number is followed by one or several note numbers [n/nn] the note number attaches to a quotation from the source being indexed. Full bibliographical details of these sources will be found in the Notes.*

Addison, Joseph 80, 81

Albigensians, medieval sect 23, 25, 26, 30

Ambrose of Milan, St 39

Angels 'of the pit', *Abbadon/ Appollyon* [*Revelation*, 9:11] 30; of light 30; of darkness, fallen 26, 30, 59; in Thomas 53, 54

Anselm of Bec, St 43

Aquinas, St Thomas 35, 49–55, 58, 59, 83, 105, 107, 109, 119, 123; *Summa Theologica* 49, 50, 52 n6, 120; *Summa contra Gentiles* 51 n5; *On Creation* 120

Aristotle 50, 52

Augustine of Hippo, St 25, 34–45 *passim*, 47, 49, 50, 52, 53, 59, 70, 105, 107, 109, 113, 123; *City of God* 43 n7, 43–4 n9, 44 n10, 49, 113; concept and practice of love in 34–5, 38, 45; *Confessions* 36 n3, 39, 40; *Enchiridion* 40; the Manichee 36; mystery of evil in 41–5, 51; the Neoplatonist 37, 38, 41

Aulen, Gustav, *Christus Victor* (1931) 114–15 nn15, 16

Barr, James, Read-Tuckwell Lectures 8 n8, 9

Barth, Karl, *Die kirchliche Dogmatik* [*Church Dogmatics*] xiii, 104, 105 n1; volume three, question

of evil in (1960) 105–7
nn2–6; *Der Romerbrief*
[*Letter to the Romans*] (1919)
104

Baudelaire, Charles 94–103
*passim*, 116, 125, 126; *Les
Fleurs du Mal* (1857) 97, 98,
n13, 99 n14, 100 n16;
Praz, Mario on, in *The
Romantic Agony* (1954) 94
n7, 95 n9, 96 nn11, 12

Blake, William 62 n1, 64, 70,
75, 87, 95–6 n10; 'On
*Paradise Lost*', in *The
Marriage of Heaven and Hell*
(1791) 62

Boethius, Anicius Manlius
Severinus 50; *Consolations
of Philosophy* 54

Bond, Edward xi

Bowra, Maurice, 'Milton and
the Destiny of Man', *From
Virgil to Milton* (1945) 66
n7, 71–2 n12

Bultmann, Rudolf 32; *Jesus
Christ and Mythology*
(1960) 31 n3

Burnaby, John, *Amor Dei*
(1938) 42 n6

Calderón de la Barca, Pedro,
*El magico prodigioso* 62

Calvin, John 58

Campbell, Joseph, *The Masks
of God* (1959) 5–6 n6

Camus, Albert 1, 2, 13, 127;
*L'Etranger* (1942); Engl.

transl. (1962) 1; *La Peste*
(1947); Engl. transl. (1982)
1–3 nn1–4, 11, 13, 18, 52,
54, 76, 78, 83, 93, 121

Chadwick, Owen, *The
Secularization of the
European Mind* (1985) 90
n1, 92 n5, 124 nn1, 2

Dante Alighieri 55–61, 67,
74, 101–2; *The Divine
Comedy* 45, 49, 55, 60, 102,
123; *Inferno* 57 nn7, 8,
57–61 *passim*, 101, 123;
*Paradiso*, 56, 123; Satan in
59–60

Darwin, Charles Robert 93,
100, 130; *The Origin of
Species by Means of Natural
Selection* (1859) 93 n6, 126,
128

Dawkins, Richard, *River Out
of Eden* (1995) 126–7 nn3,
4, 128

Descartes, René, *Discourse on
Method* (1637) 75

Dionysius 50

Dryden, John, *Song for St
Cecilia's Day* (1687) 79, 80,
81, 85

Duns Scotus, John 70

Eliot, T. S. [Thomas Stearns],
*Four Quartets* (1944) xiii;
'Baudelaire' in *Selected
Essays* (1951) 102 nn18,
19, 103 n20; Introduction

to Charles Williams: *All Hallows' Eve* 108

Evans, Gillian R., *Augustine on Evil* (1982) 38 nn4, 5, 43

Frye, Northrop, *Creation and Recreation* (1980) 6, 7 n6, 9

Gardner, Helen, *Religion and Literature* (1971) 129 n5

Grotius, Hugo 62

Hadfield, Alice Mary 123

Hesiod: Pandora, myth of 4–5 n5, 9, 10

Hooker, Richard, *Laws of Ecclesiastical Polity* (1594) 73–4

Hussey, Christopher, *The Picturesque* (1927) 95 n8

Innocent III, pope 23

Islam 41

Jerome, St (properly, Eusebius Sophronius Hieronymus): Vulgate version of the scriptures 49

Jesus Christ 27, 30, 73; the Second Adam 8

Jung, Carl Gustav, *Memories, Dreams, Reflections* (1962) 13 n1

Keble, John, *The Christian Year* (1827) 89, 90

Kierkegaard, Søren, published by Oxford University Press 104

Law, William, *A Serious Call to a Holy and Devout Life* (1728) 84–5 n5

Le Goff, Jacques, 'Medieval Man', *The Medieval World* (1990) 47 n2

Leibniz, Gottfried Wilhelm 78, 82, 83, 88; *Essais de théodicée* (1710) 78, 82, 92

Lewis, C. S. [Clive Staples], *Broadcast Talks* (1942) [repr. in *Mere Christianity* (1952)] 26–7 n2, 32; *Preface to Paradise Lost* (1963) 68 n10, 69, 73; *The Allegory of Love* (1936) 46 n1; *The Problem of Pain* (1957) 116–17

Lisbon, earthquake of 1755 76, 82

Locke, John, *Essay concerning Human Understanding* (1690) 75

Manicheeism 25, 26, 30, 36–7, 46, 47, 101

Marlowe, Christopher, *The Tragical History of Dr Faustus* (1604) 62

Milton, John 62–75 *passim*, 79, 85, 112, 113, 118–19; *Areopagitica* (1644) 69, 72, 73, 112, 117 n19, 118; on Edmund Spenser, Duns

Scotus and Thomas in 70; *De Doctrina Christiana*; publ. posth. (1823) 63; *Paradise Lost* (compl. 1665; pubd 1667) 45, 62, 63–4 n4, 63–75 *passim*, 65 n5, 66 n6, 67–8 n8, 68 n9, 74 n13, 112, 113; *Paradise Regained* (1671) 71, 72–3; on Christ as mirror of Adam and Satan in 72–3; *Samson Agonistes* (1671) 71; *Selected Prose*, ed. C. A. Patrides, 70 n11

Montfort, Simon de 23

Neil, William, 'Christian humanism' in *The Christian Faith in Art* (1966) 49 n4

New Testament, books of [references in *italics*]: *1 Corinthians, 15:21* 8; *1 Peter, 2:20* 19; *2 Thessalonians, 2:7* 9; *St Luke, 10:18* 27, 30; *Revelation, 9:11, 12:7* 30; *Romans* 28–9; *8:20–22* 29; dualistic cosmic myth in 28, 31

Newman, John Henry 7

Newton, Isaac 79, 80, 81, 82; *Philosophiae Naturalis Principia Mathematica* (1687) 80, 82

Nietzsche, Friedrich 125, 127; *Beyond Good and Evil* (1888) 124; *The Gay Science* (1882) 124

Old Testament, books of [references in *italics*]: *Daniel* 27; *Deuteronomy* 7, 16–17; *Ecclesiastes, 1:9* 21–2; *9:12* 22; *Enoch* 27; *Genesis* 6, *2:8* 5; *2:15* 6; *2:25* 7; *3:1–7* 7, 118; *3:16* 9–10; Fall of Man, myth of 7–8, 10, 130–31; interpretation of by Charles Williams 110, 113–14; *Isaiah, 45:5–7* 28; *Job* 12–22 *passim*, 27, 55, 82, 83, 86, 121, 122, 127; *19:6–14* 14; *8:5–14* 14; *ch. 24* 15; *33:14–16* 18; *33:19, 29–30* 19; *38:3* 20; *42:6* 21; *Zechariah* 27

Pandora, myth of, *see Hesiod*

Paul, St, apostle, *see New Testament, books of*

Pope, Alexander 80; *Essay on Man* (1734) 85–6 nn7–10, 87; Nuttall, A. D., Preface to edn of (1984) 85 n6, 86, 87 n11

Priestley, J. B. [John Boynton], *Literature and Western Man* (1980) 101 n17

Quennell, Peter Courtney,

*Baudelaire and the Symbolists* (1954) 100 n15

Renan, (Joseph) Ernest 90, 92, 94, 100, 103; *L'Avenir de la Science* 91; *La Vie de Jésus* (1863) 89–90, 91, 92; Chadwick, Owen, on fame of in *Secularization of the European Mind* (1985) 90, 92; quoted in Reardon, B., *Religion in the Age of Romanticism* (1985) 90 n2, 91 nn3, 4

Sade, Comte de (known as Marquis) 95, 96, 99; Praz, Mario on, in *The Romantic Agony* (1954) 95, 96; *Justine* (1791) 96; *Juliette* (1798) 96

Satan: the 'accuser' 16, 27; the 'devil' 25, 26, 30, 32; the 'dragon' [*Revelation* 12:7] 30; in Augustine 44–5; in Baudelaire *Les Fleurs du Mal* 100–101; in Dante: *Inferno* 60; in Fransisco de Suarez 66; in Grotius 66; in Ireneaus and Justin 65; in *Job* 12; in medieval imagination 47; in Milton *Paradise Lost* 63–75 *passim*; in Origen 65

Sayers, Dorothy L. [Leigh], transl. of Dante; *Inferno* (1949), Introduction to 58

n9; *The Poetry of Search and the Poetry of Statement* (1963) 61 n10

Shakespeare, William, *Troilus and Cressida* 110–11 n9; *King Lear* 15

Spenser, Edmund 70

Tasso, Torquato, *Gerusalemme Liberata* [*Jerusalem Delivered*] (1575) 62

Tennyson, Alfred Lord 92

Tertullian (properly Quintus Septimus Florens Tertullianus): *Apology* 26 n1

Tillich, Paul 'Art and Society' in *On Art and Architecture* (1952) xii

Vardy, Peter, *The Puzzle of Evil* (1992) 33 n4

Virgil, with Dante in the *Inferno* 56–7

Voltaire (properly François-Marie Arouet de) 76, 79, 87; *Candide* (1759) 77 nn1, 2, 78 n3, 88; *Poeme sur le desastre de Lisbonne* (1756) 77

Vondel, Joost van den, *Lucifer* (1654) 62

West, Rebecca, *A Celebration* (1978) 34 n1, 35 n2, 38, 50

Westfall, Richard S., *Science and Religion in Seventeenth-*

*Century England* (1958) 80 n4

Williams, Charles (Walter Stansby) 67, 68, 69, 71, 73, 104, 107–23 *passim*; *All Hallows' Eve* (USA edn., 1981) 108 n7; *He Came Down From Heaven* (1938) 110, 112, 113, nn12–14, 114, 115–16 n17, 118 n20, 119, 122; interest in occult practice 109; *Outlines of Romantic Theology*: publ. posth. (1990) 110; *Reason and Beauty in the Poetic Mind* (1933) 110, 112 n11; *The Cross* (1943) 116, 121; *The Descent of the Dove* (1939) 24; *The English Poetic Mind* (1932) 110; *The Image of the City* (1958) 121 n22, 121–2 n23, 122 nn24, 25, 122–3 n26; *The Forgiveness of Sins* (1943) 110, 114; *The New Christian Year* (1940) 104; on Dante: *The Divine Comedy* 123; *Witchcraft* (1980) 109 n8, 111 n10, 120–21; quoting canons of 1234 in 48 n3

Wilson, A. [Andrew] N., *The Life of John Milton* (1984) 63 n2, 64 n4

Wilson, Edmund 60

Wood, James, *Job and the Human Situation* (1966) 21 n3